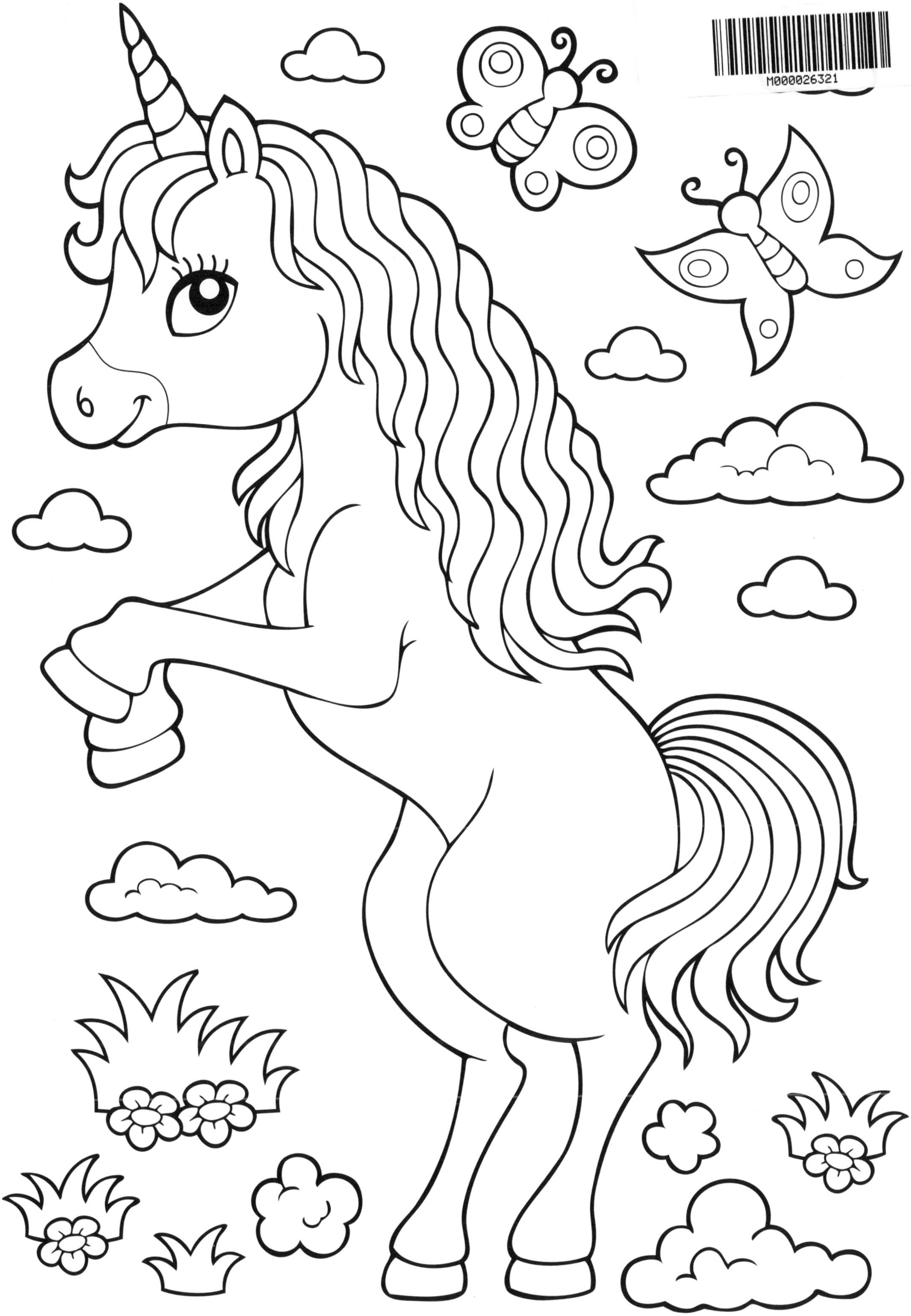

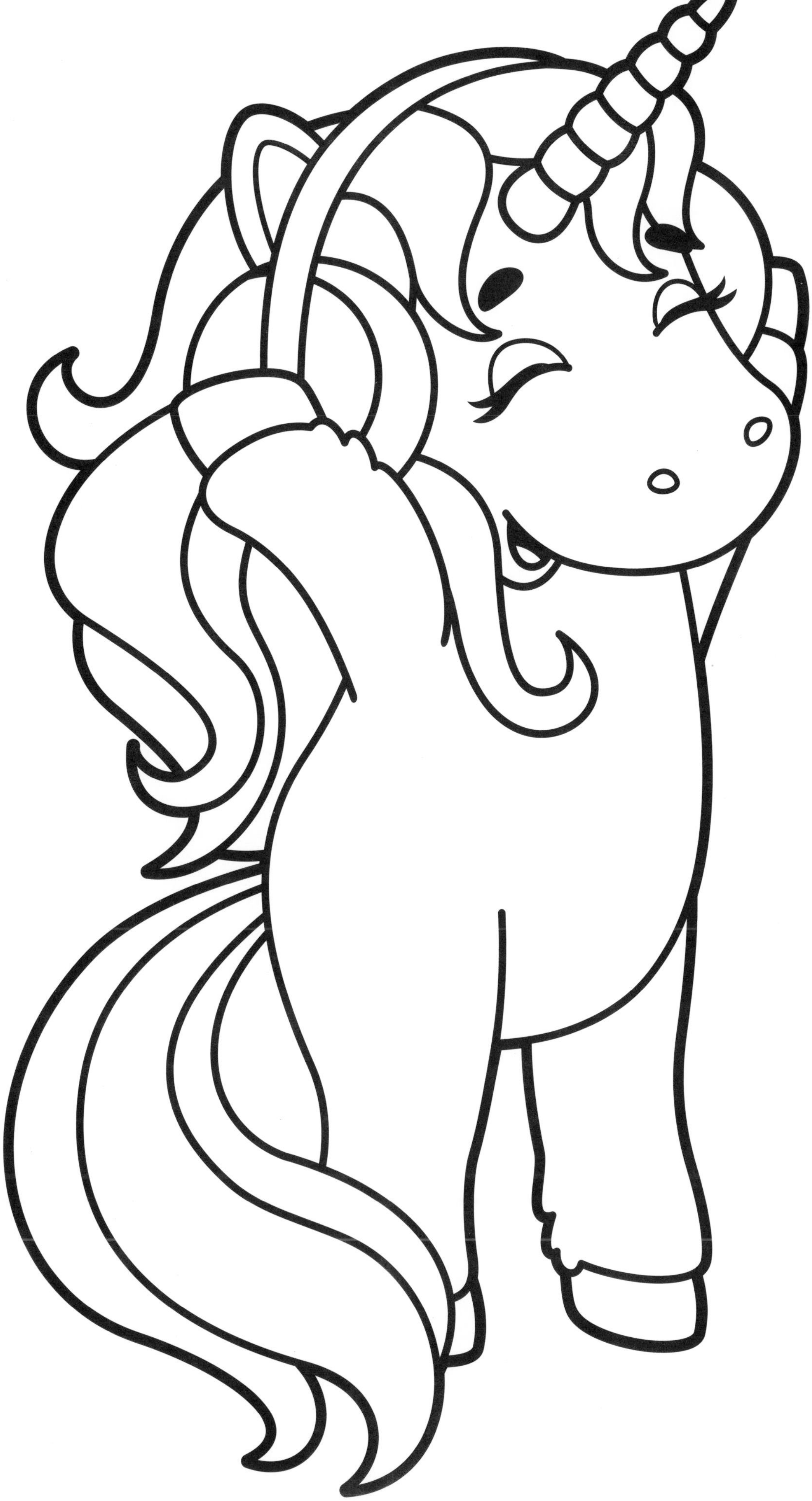

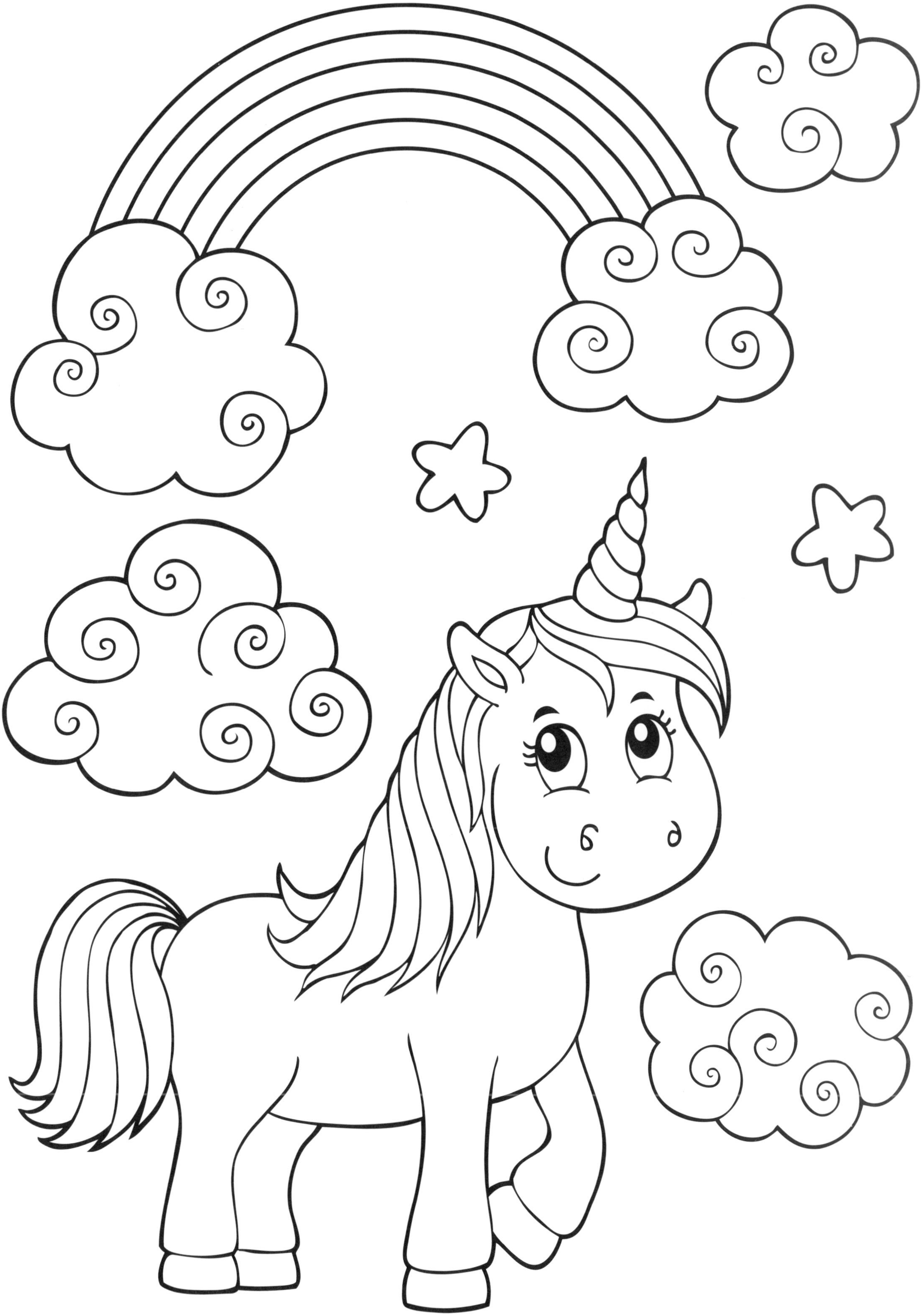

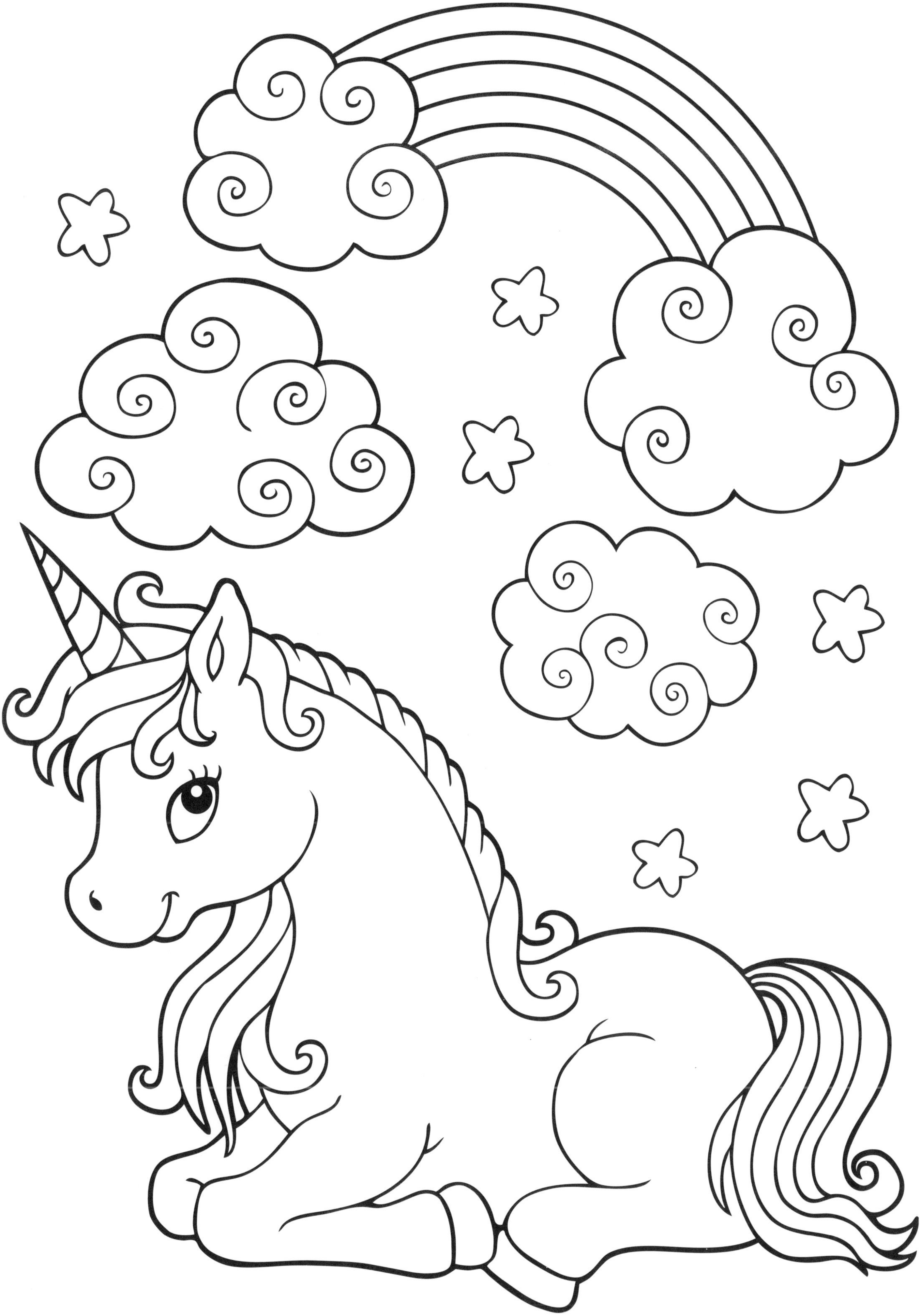

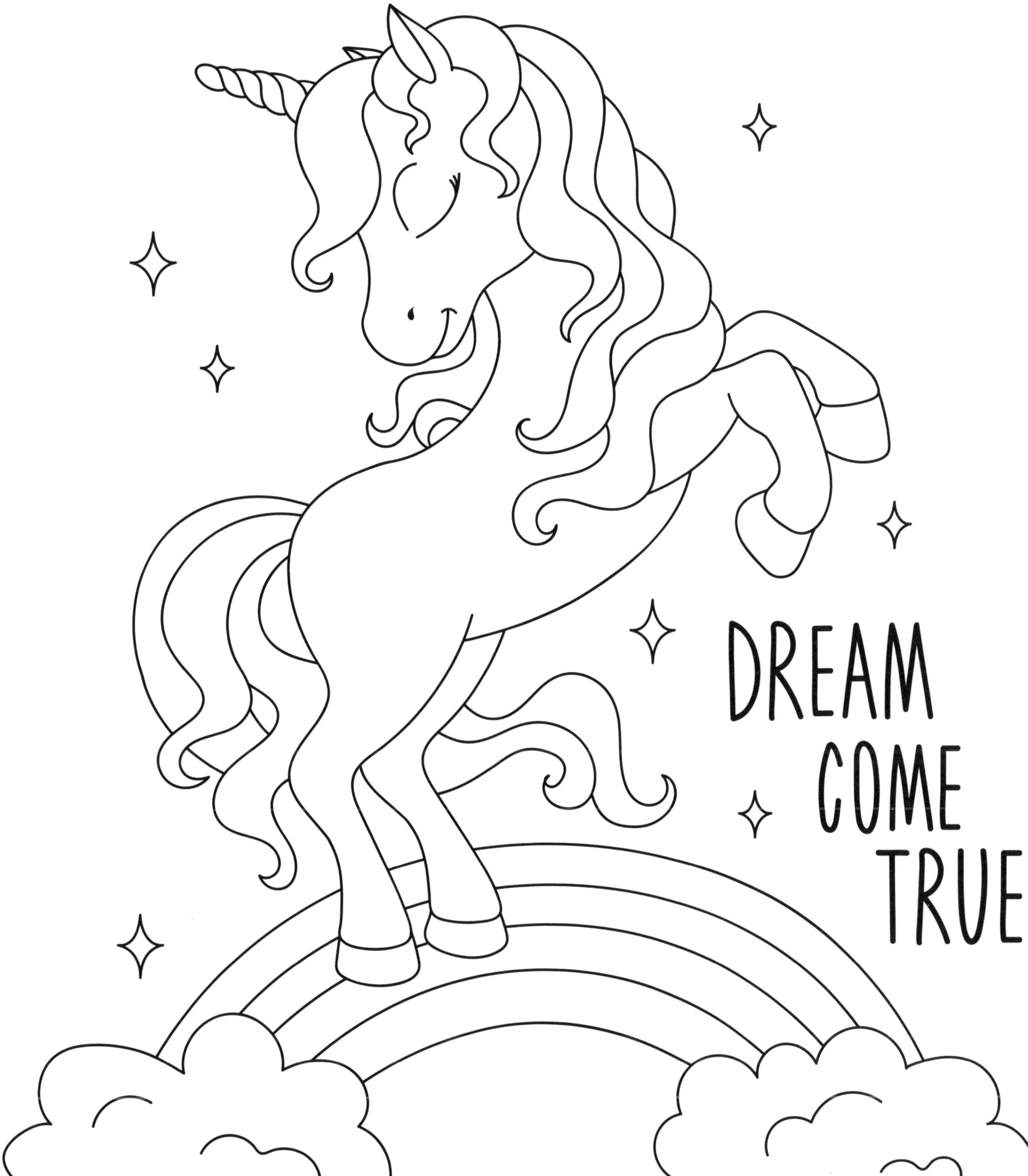
DREAM
COME
TRUE

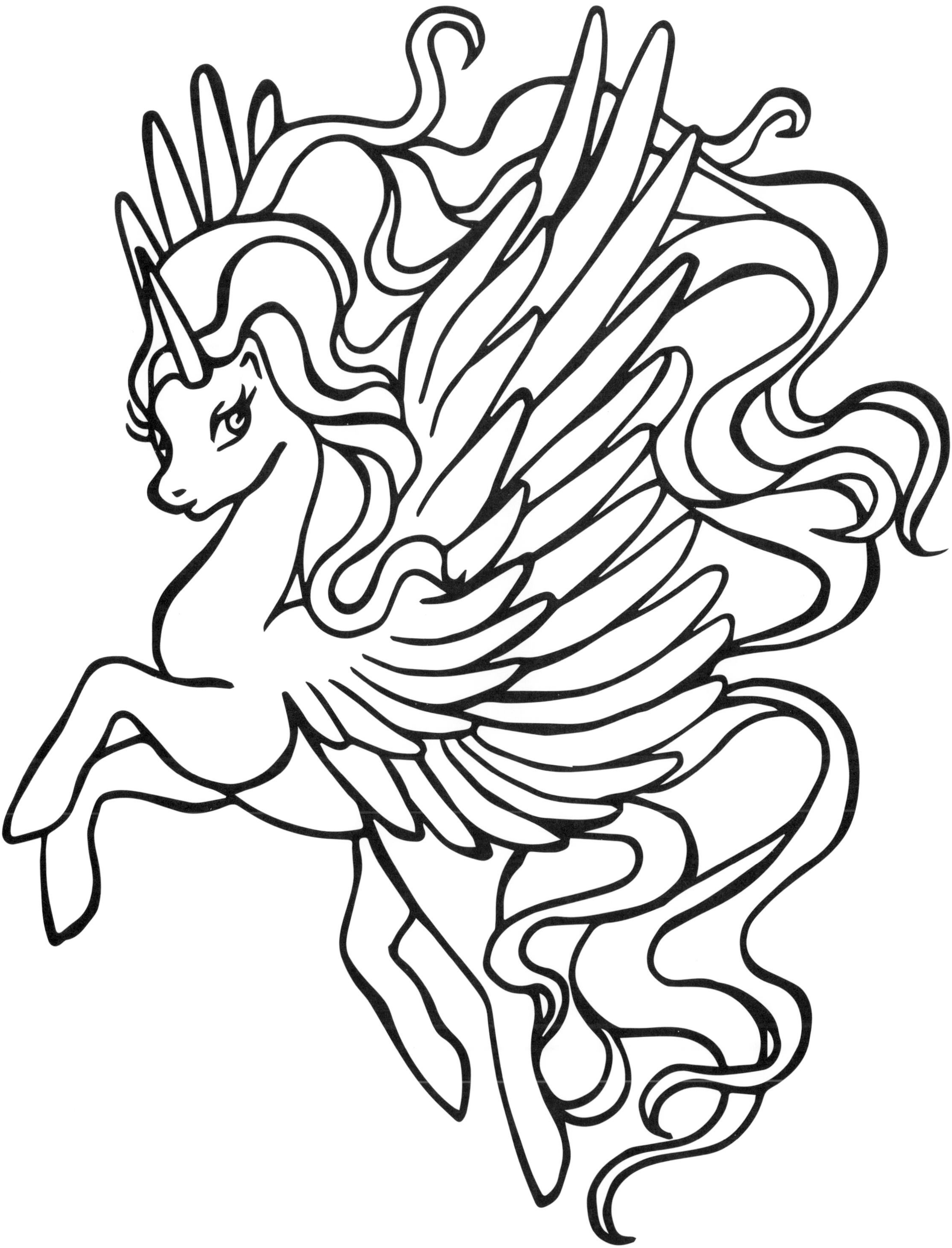

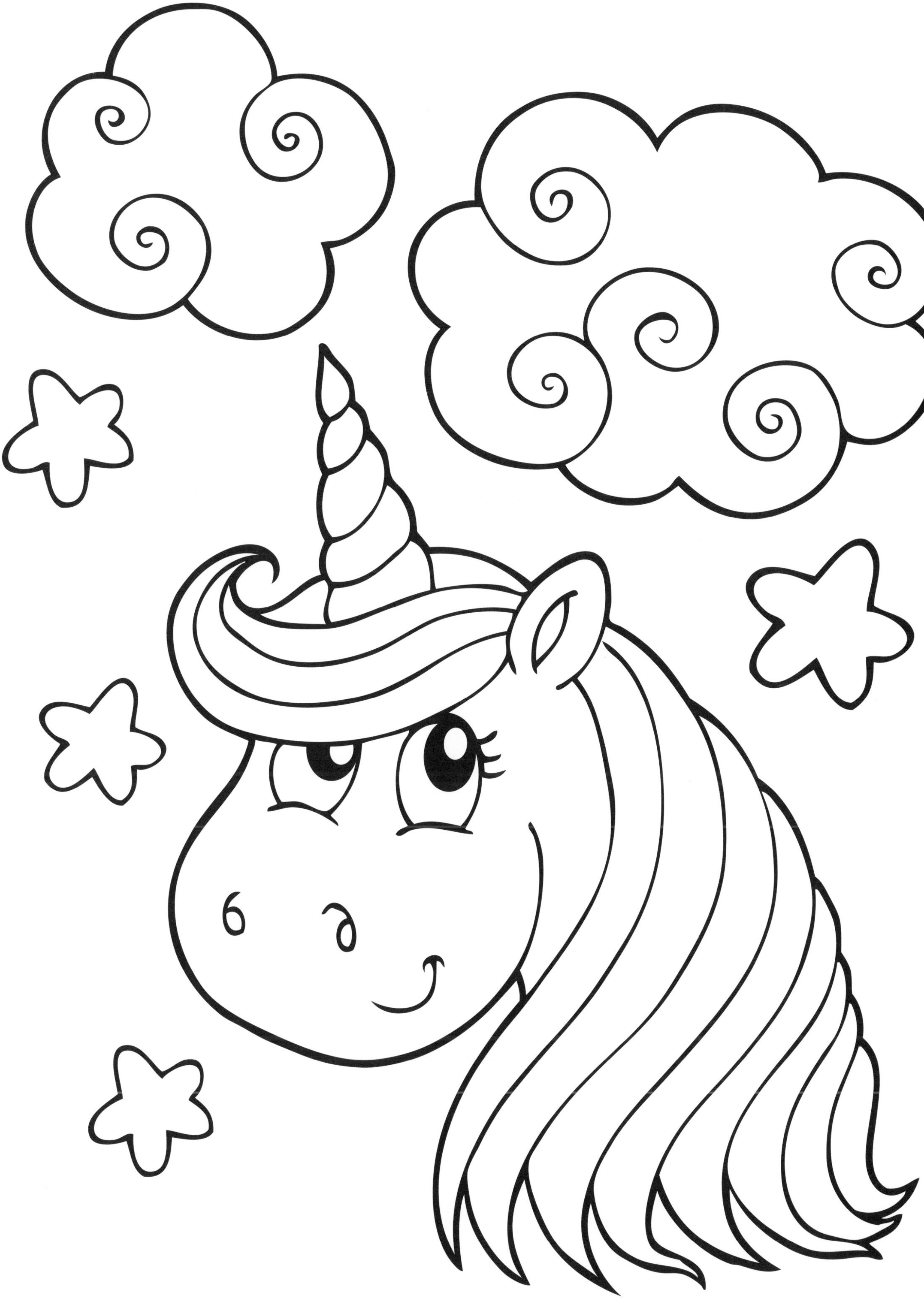

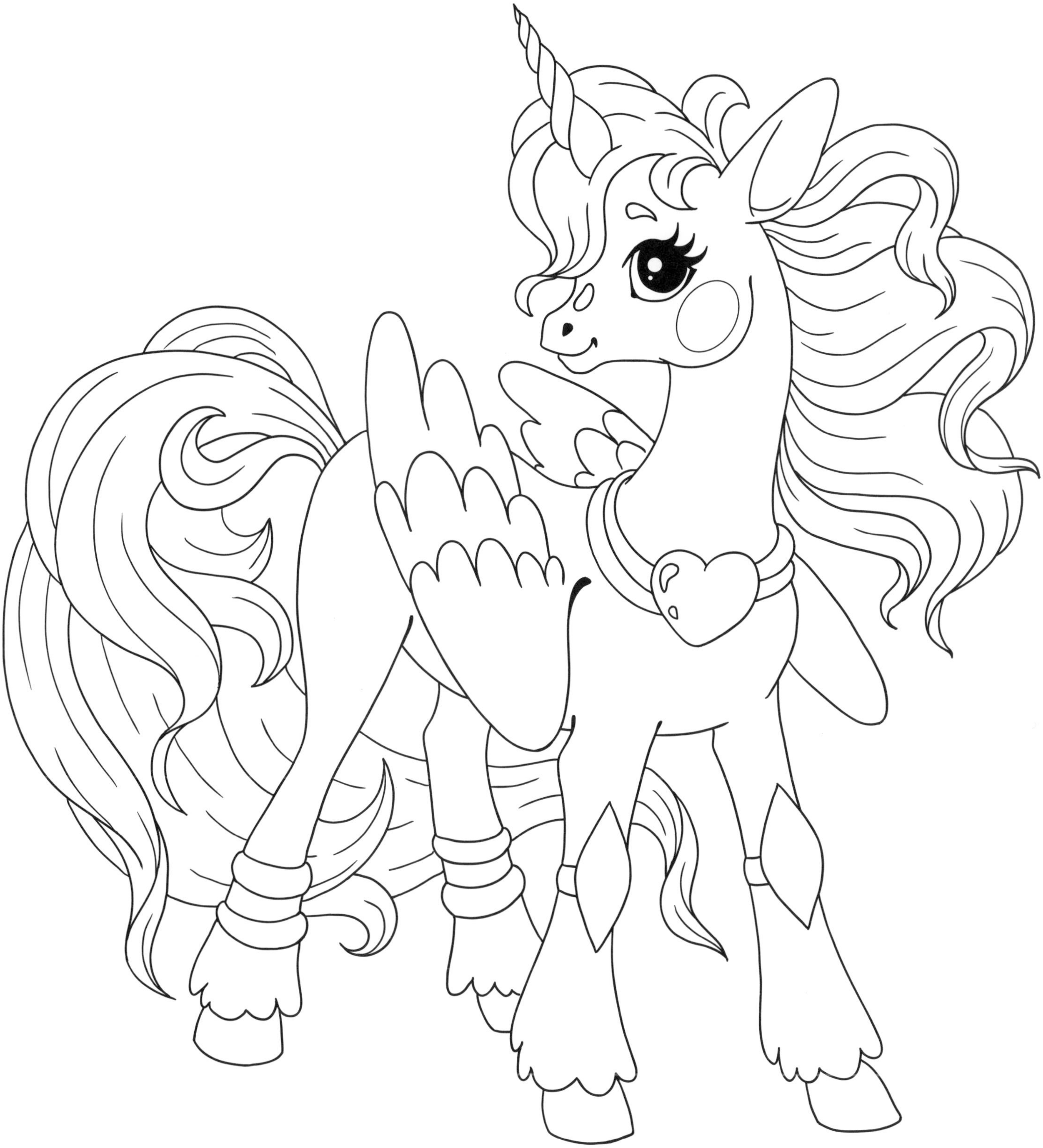

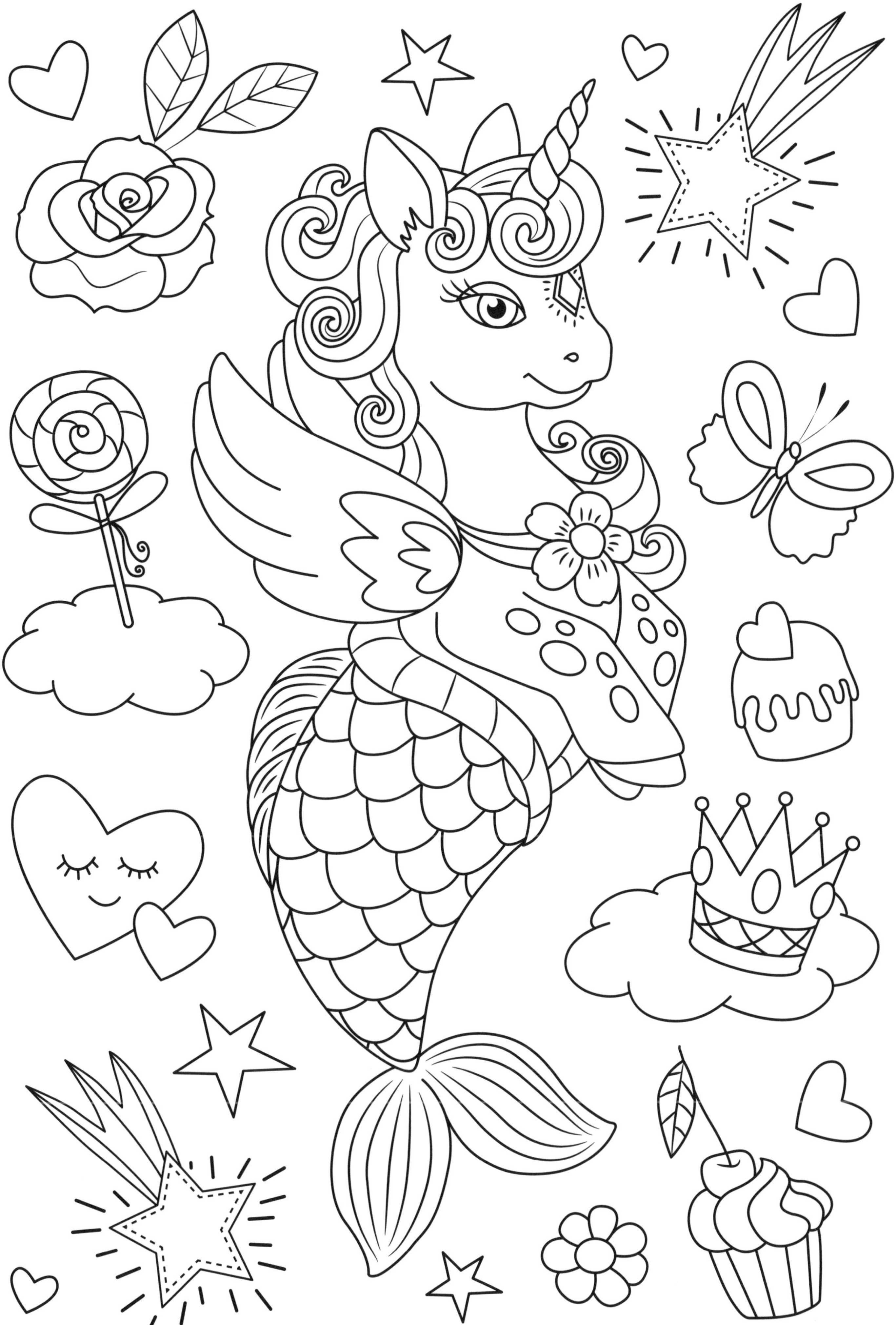

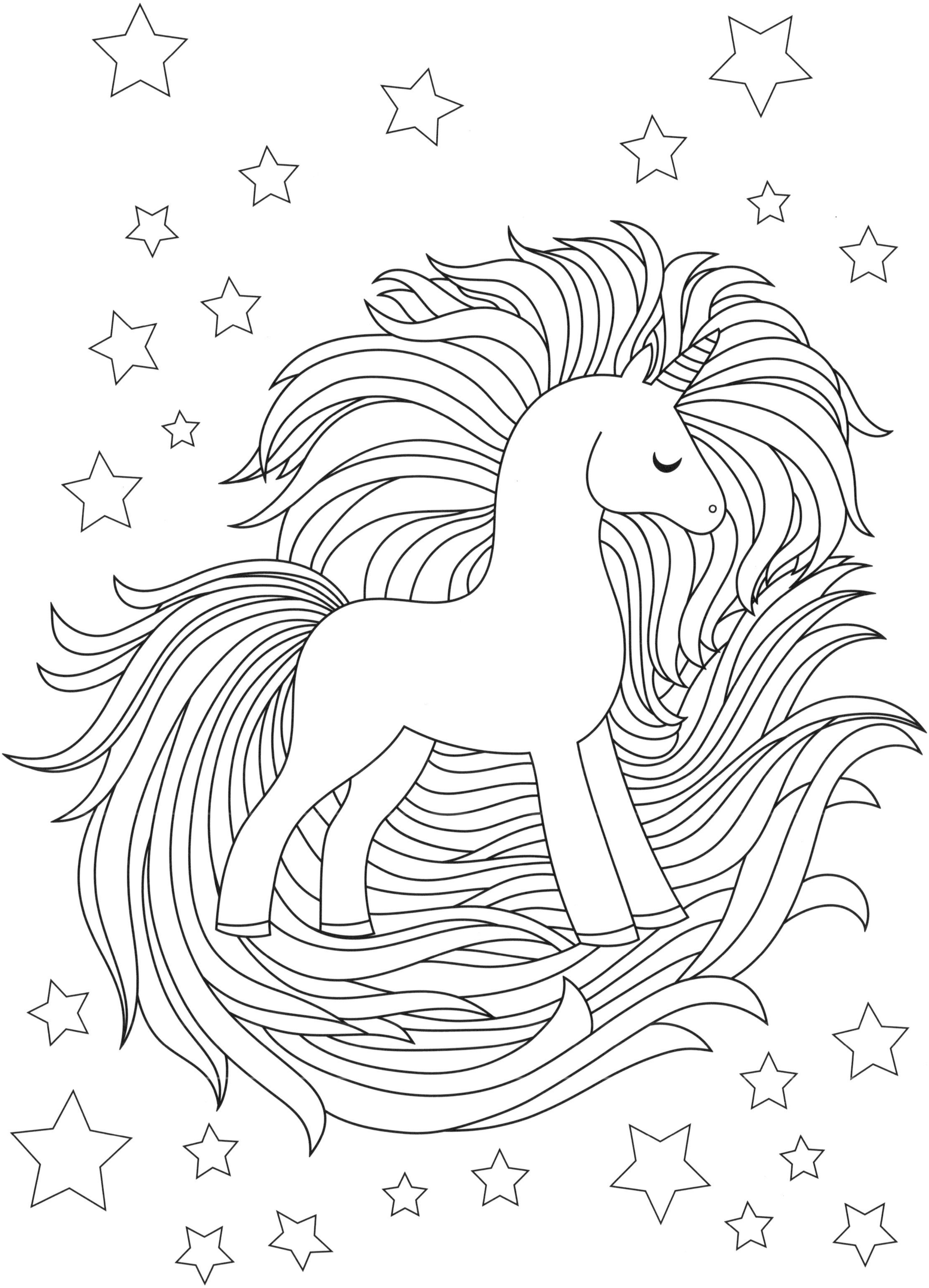

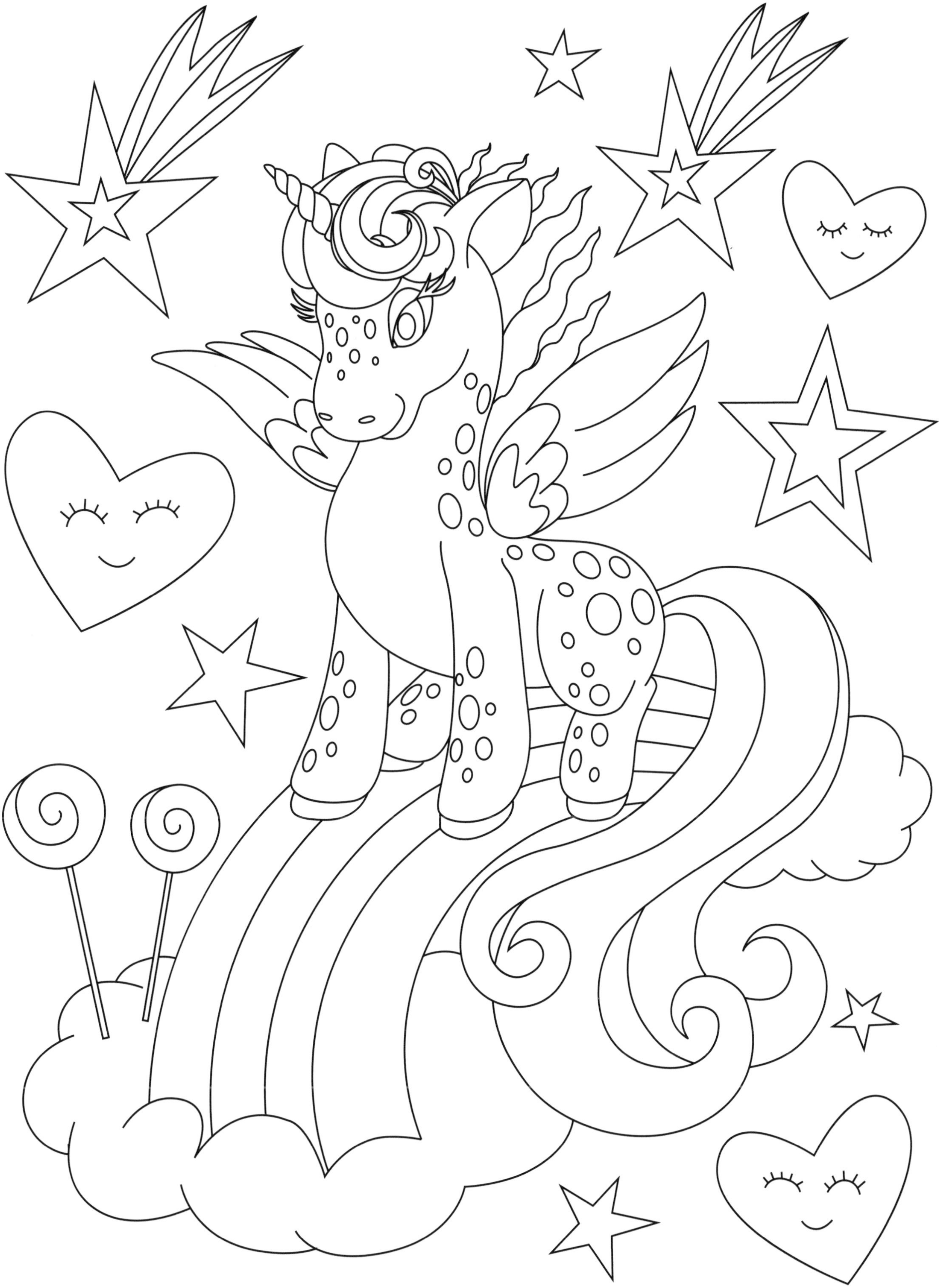

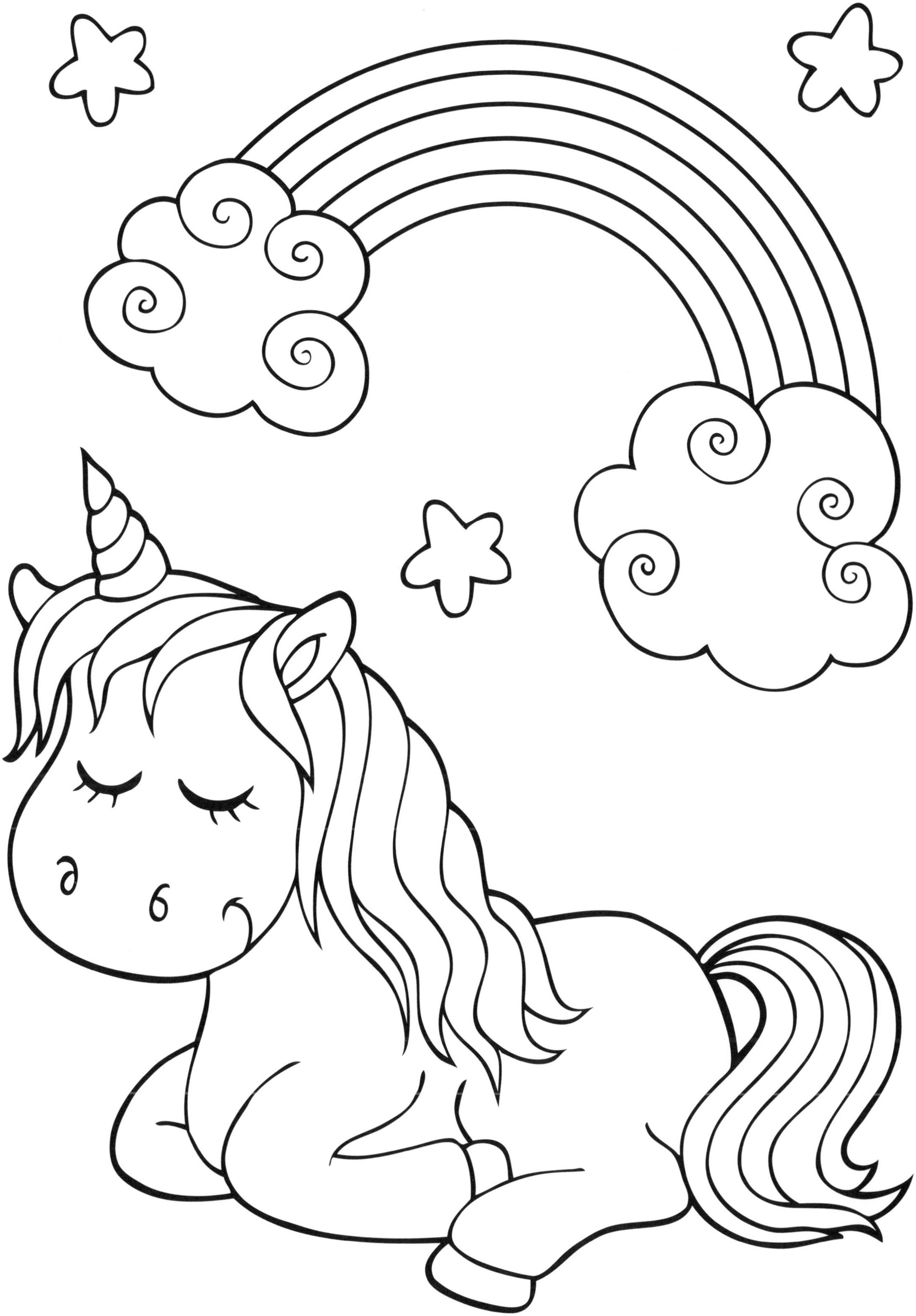

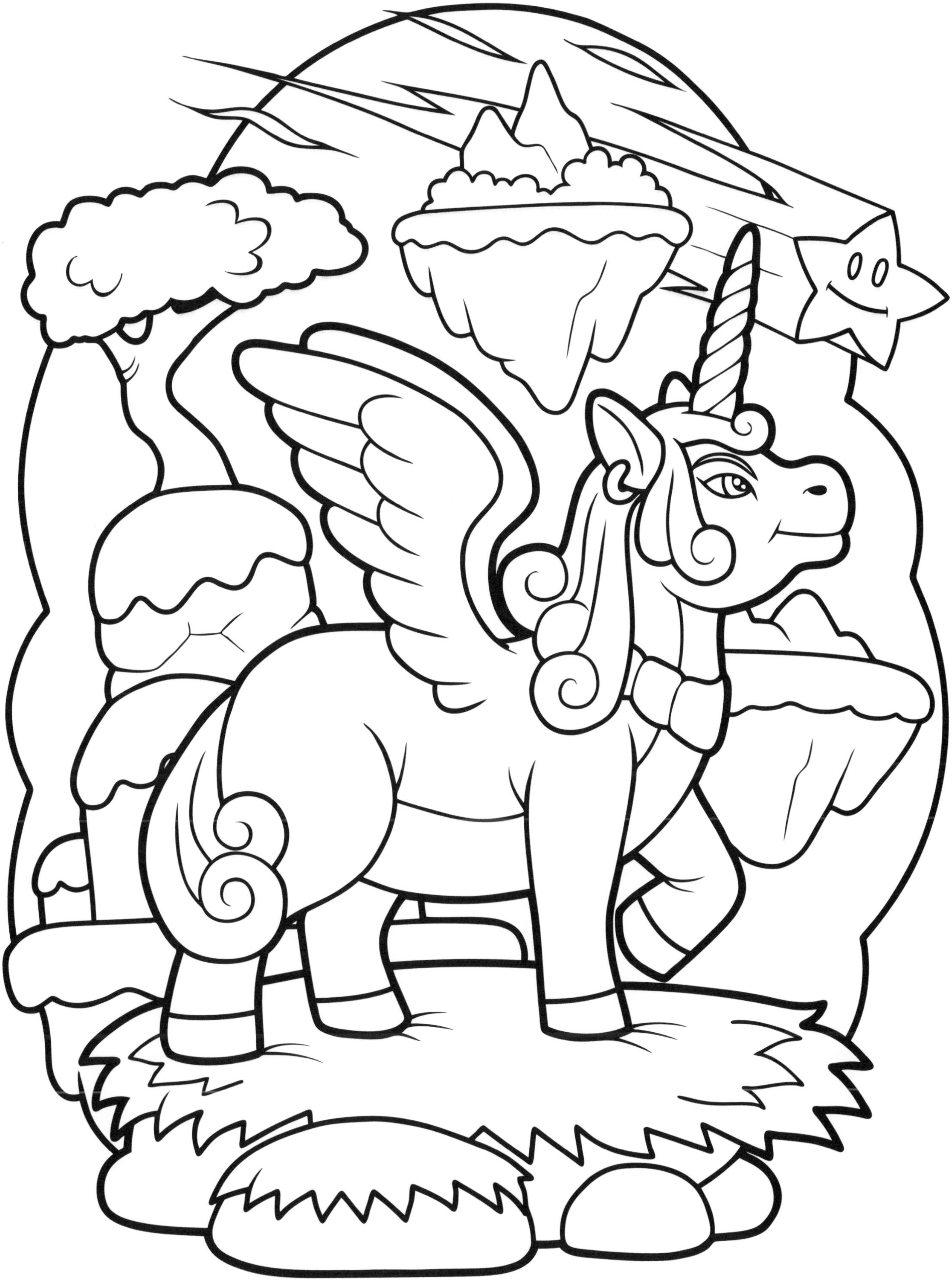

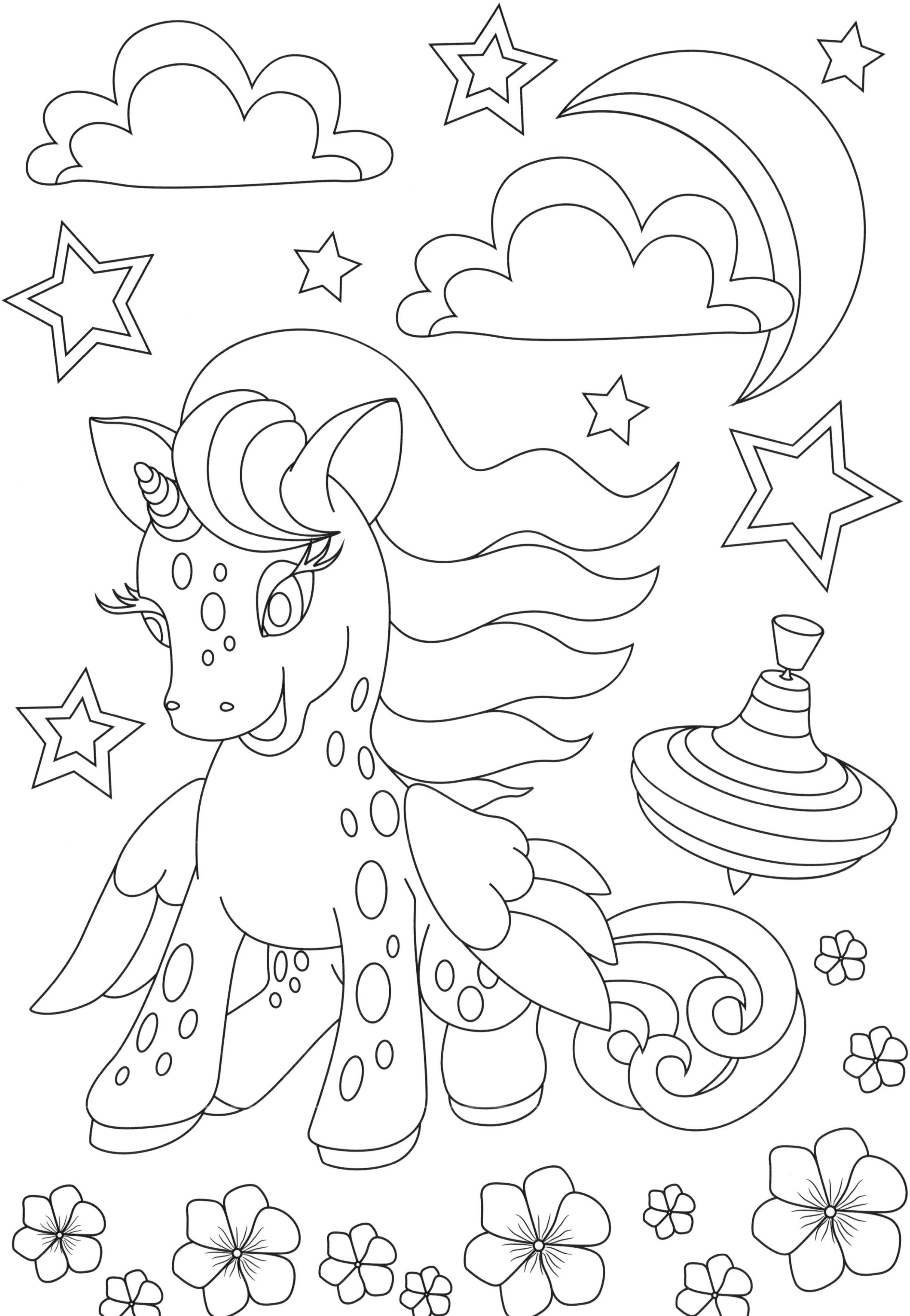

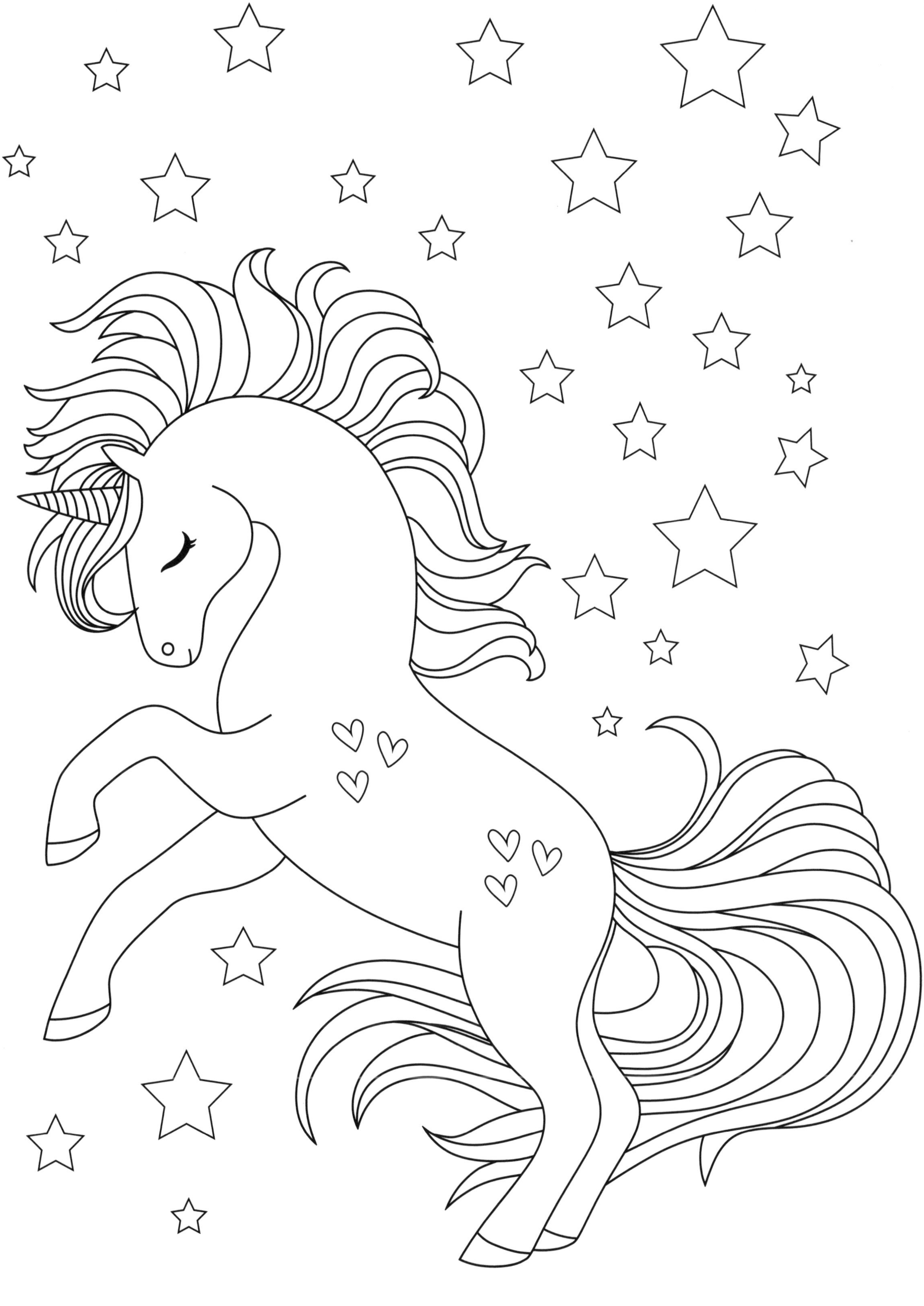

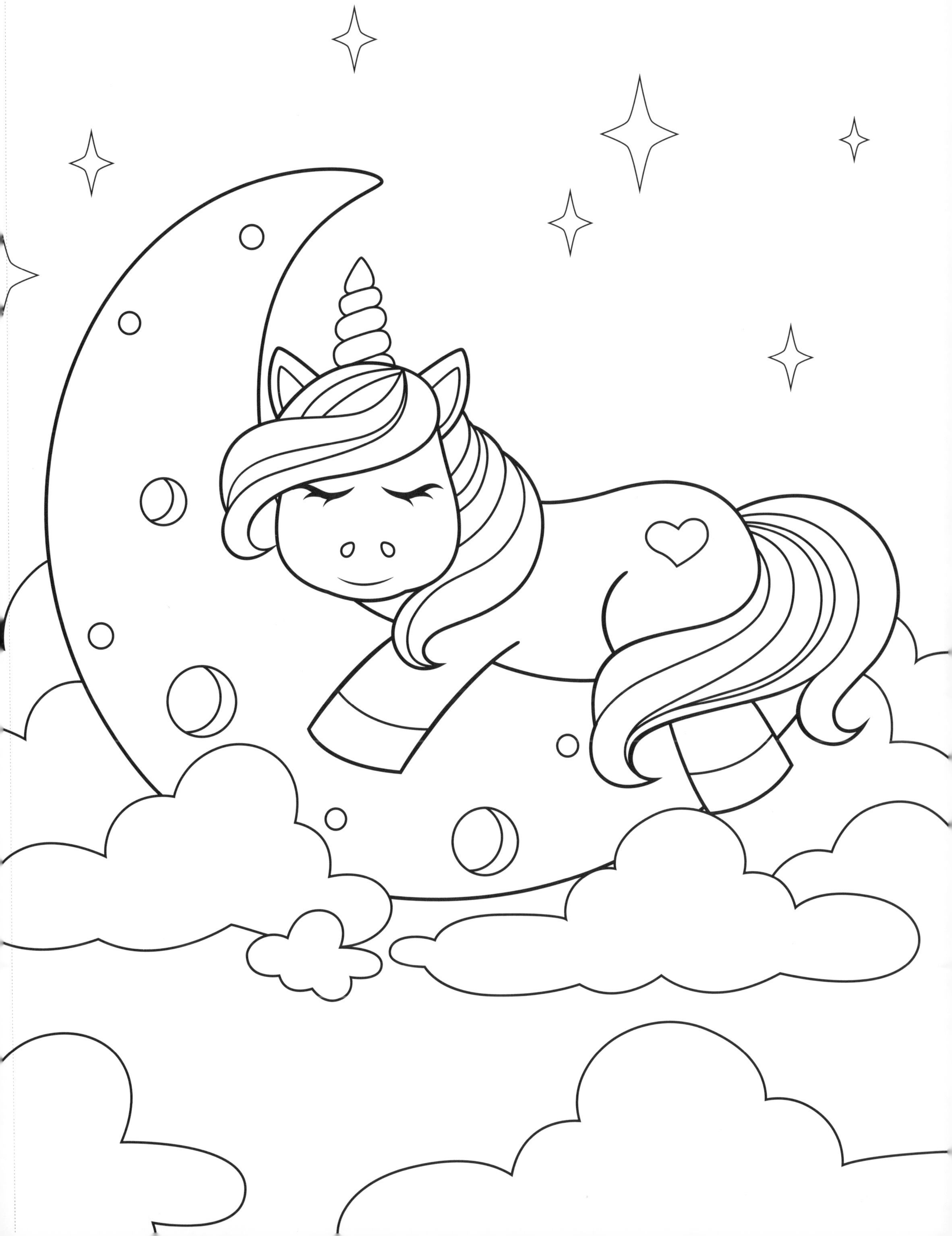

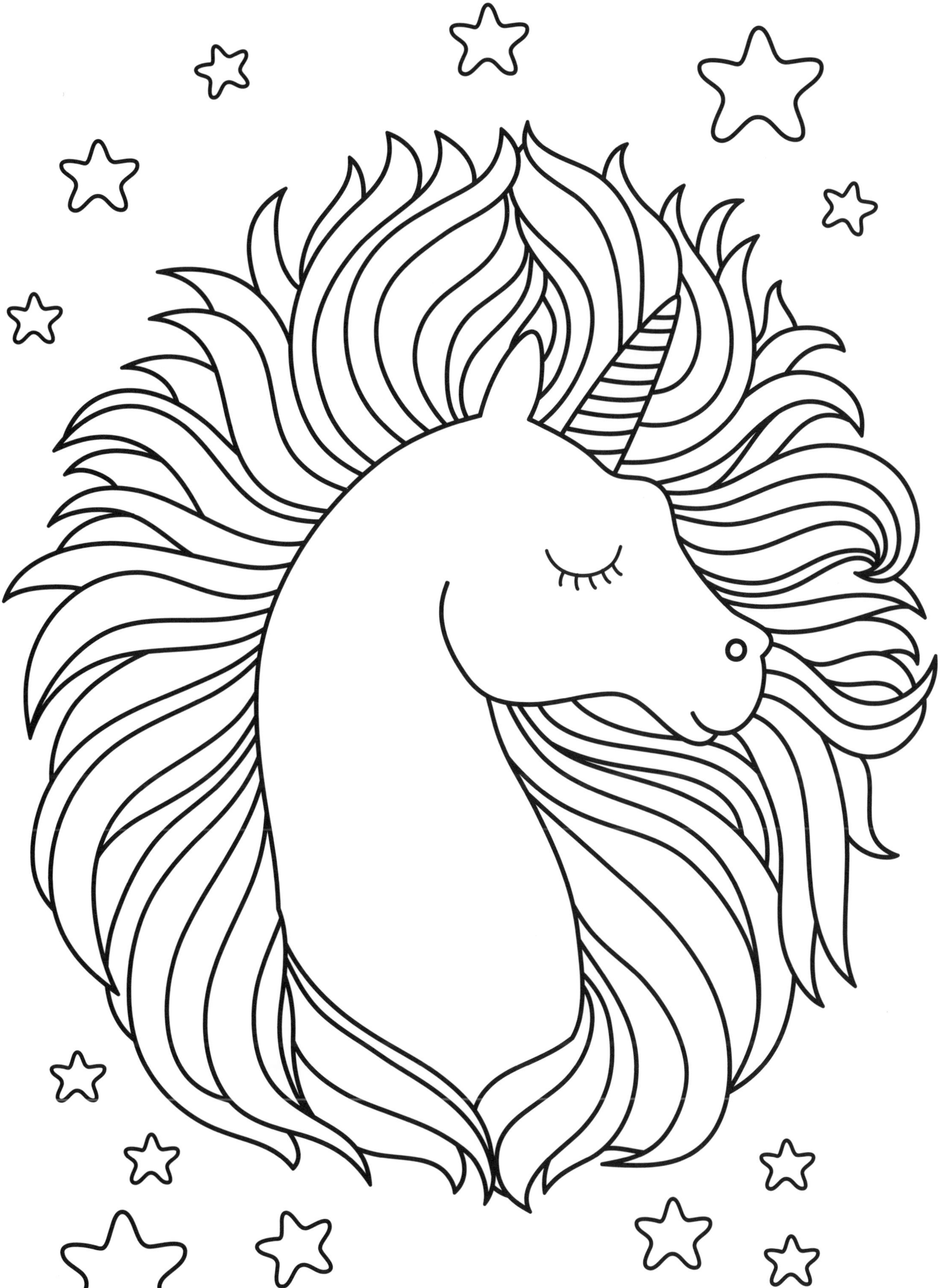

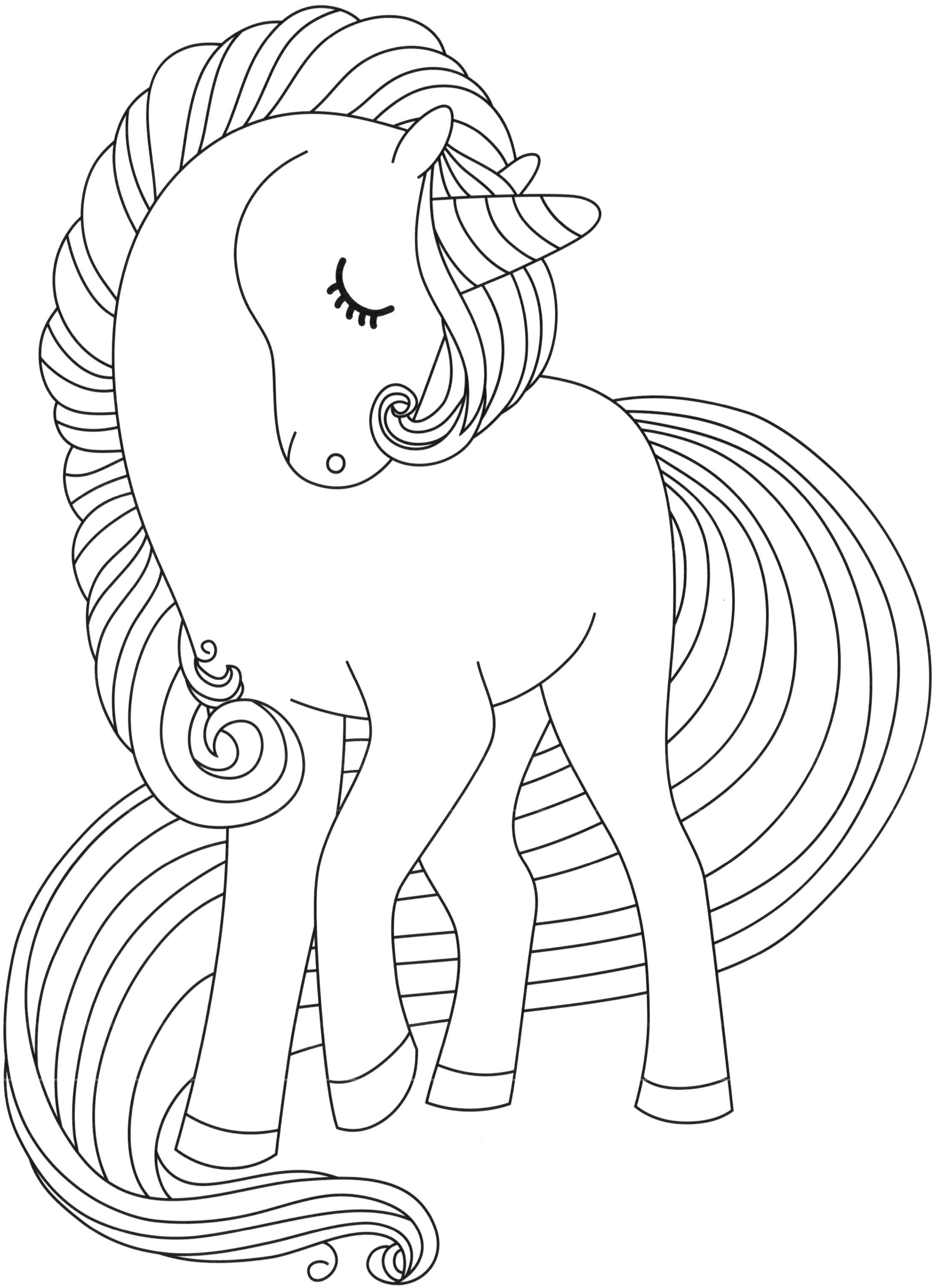

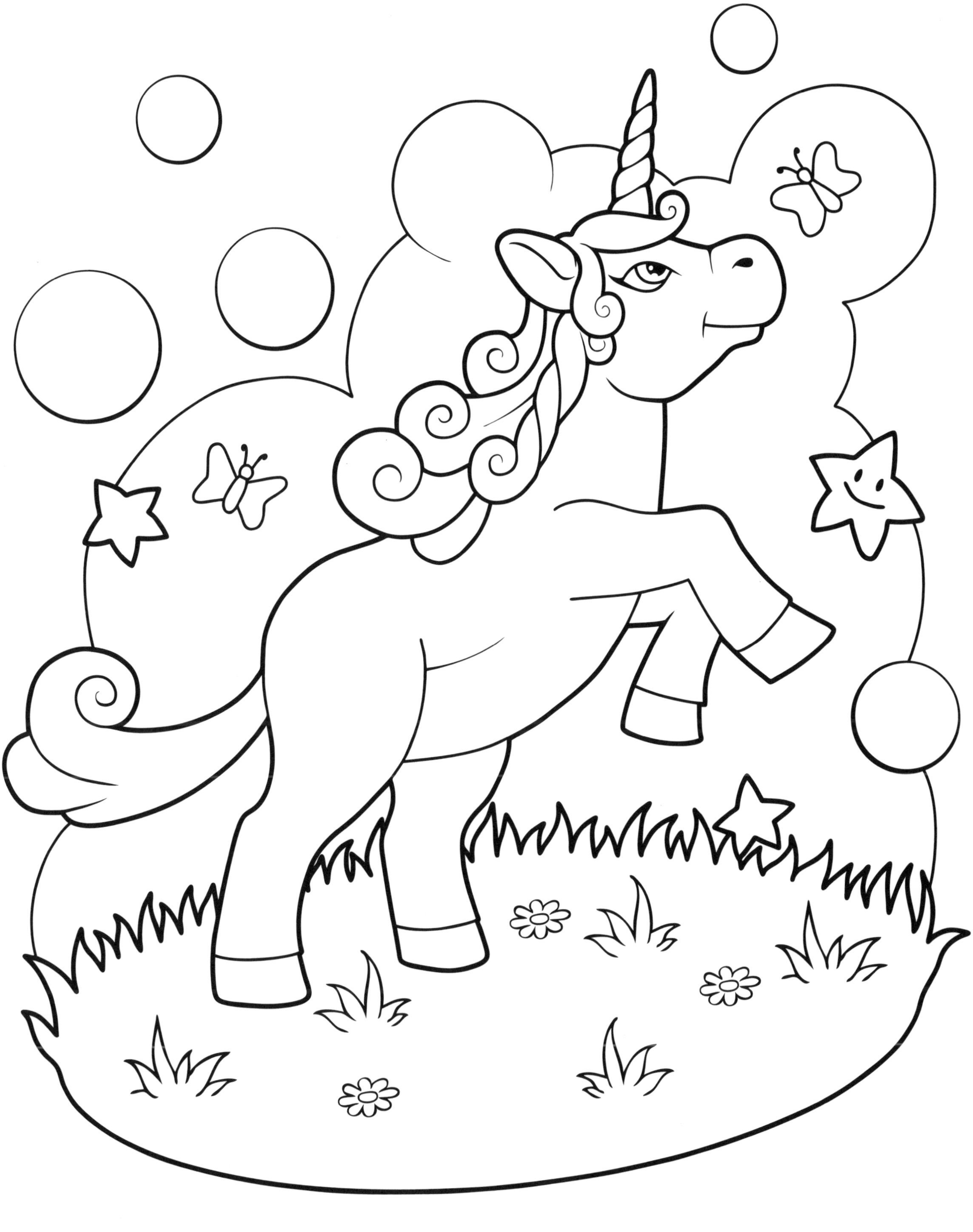

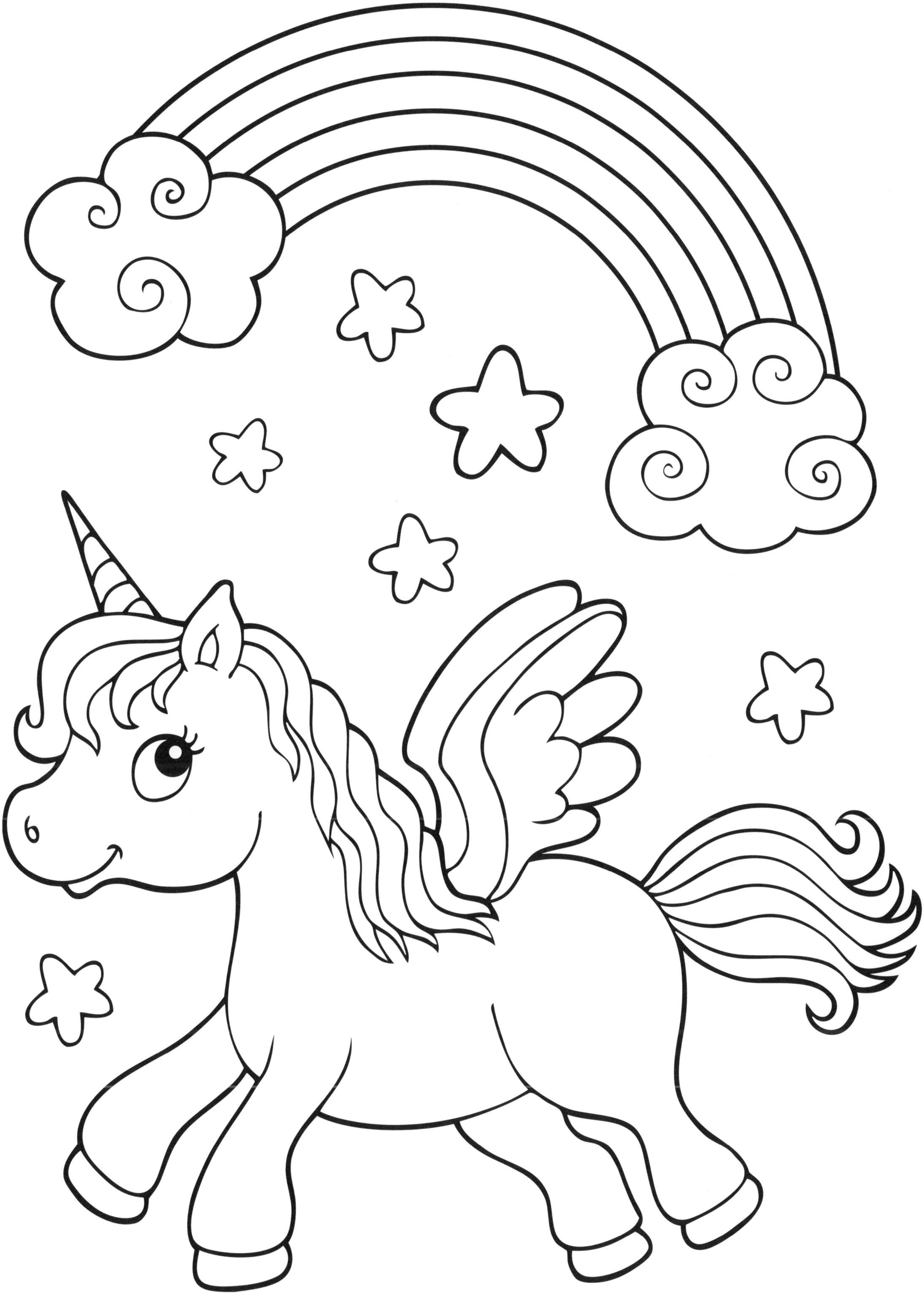

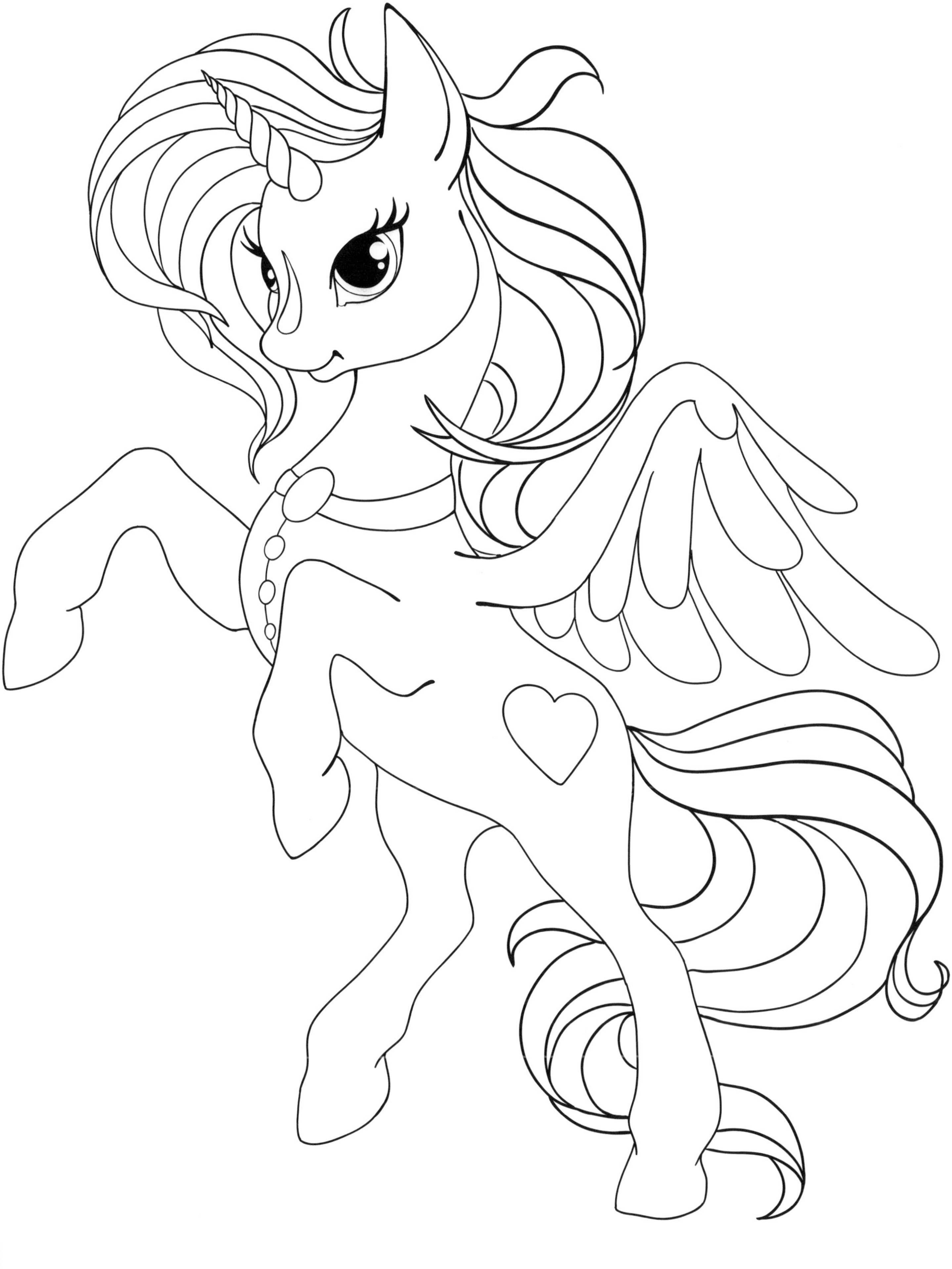

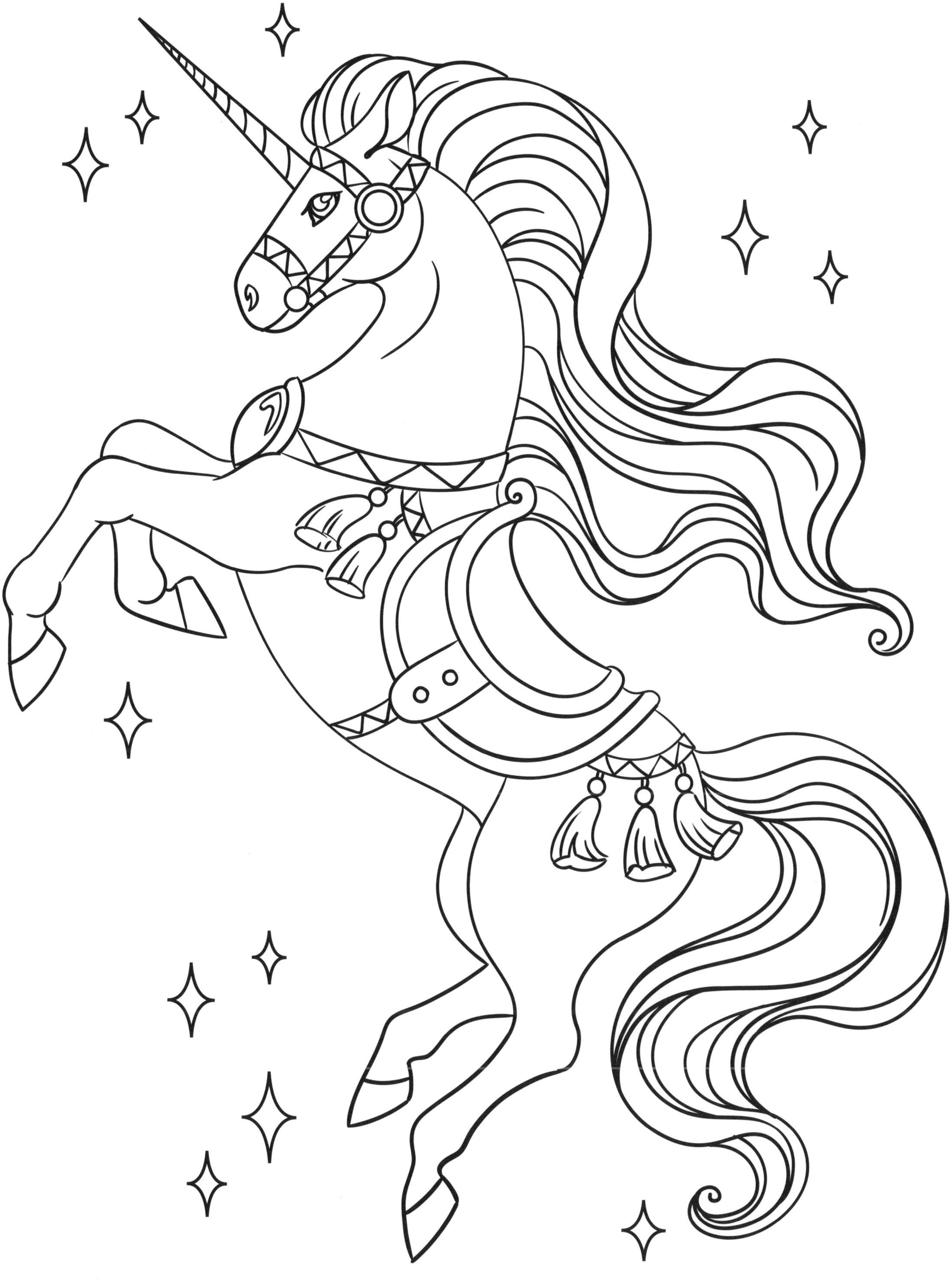

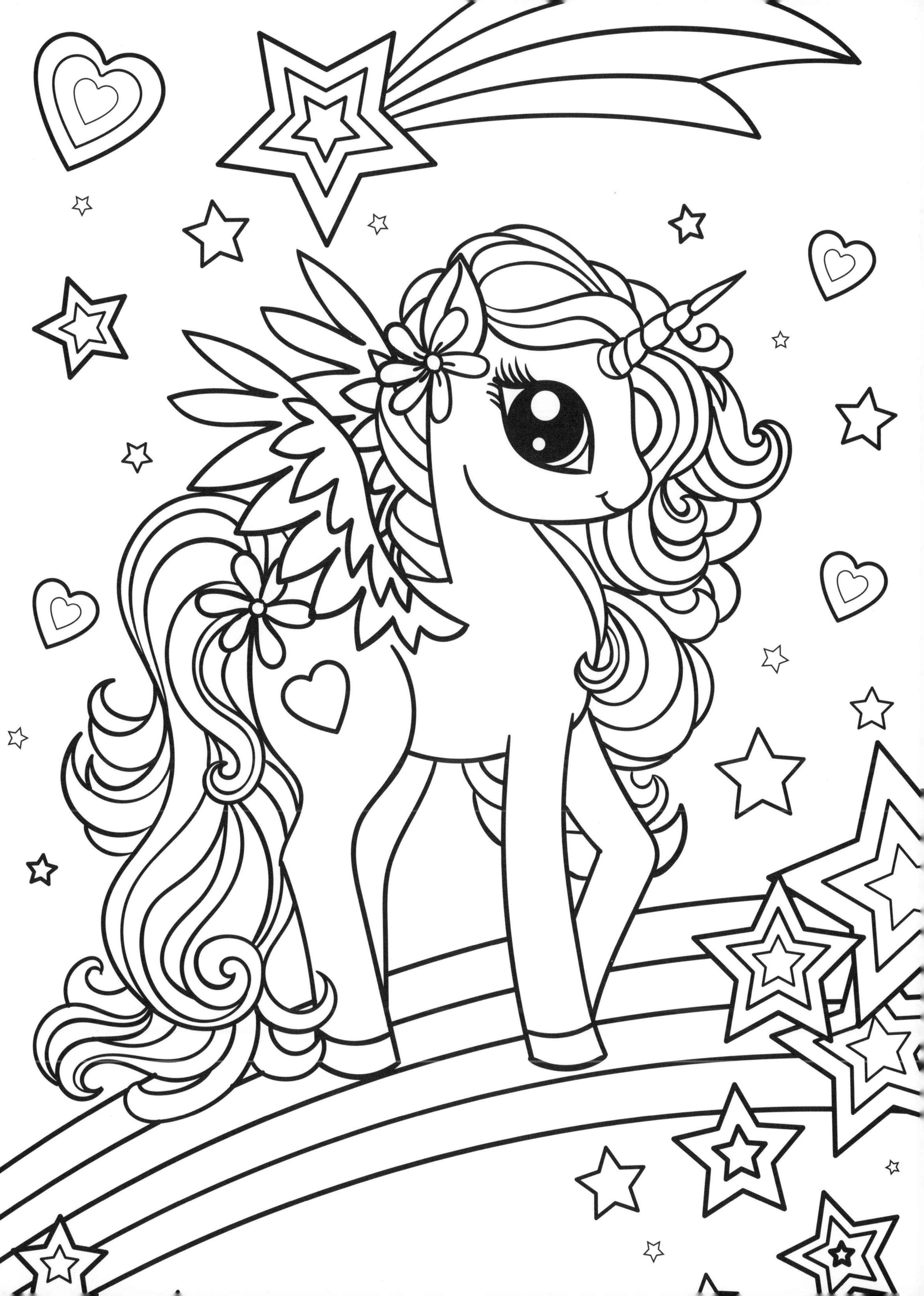

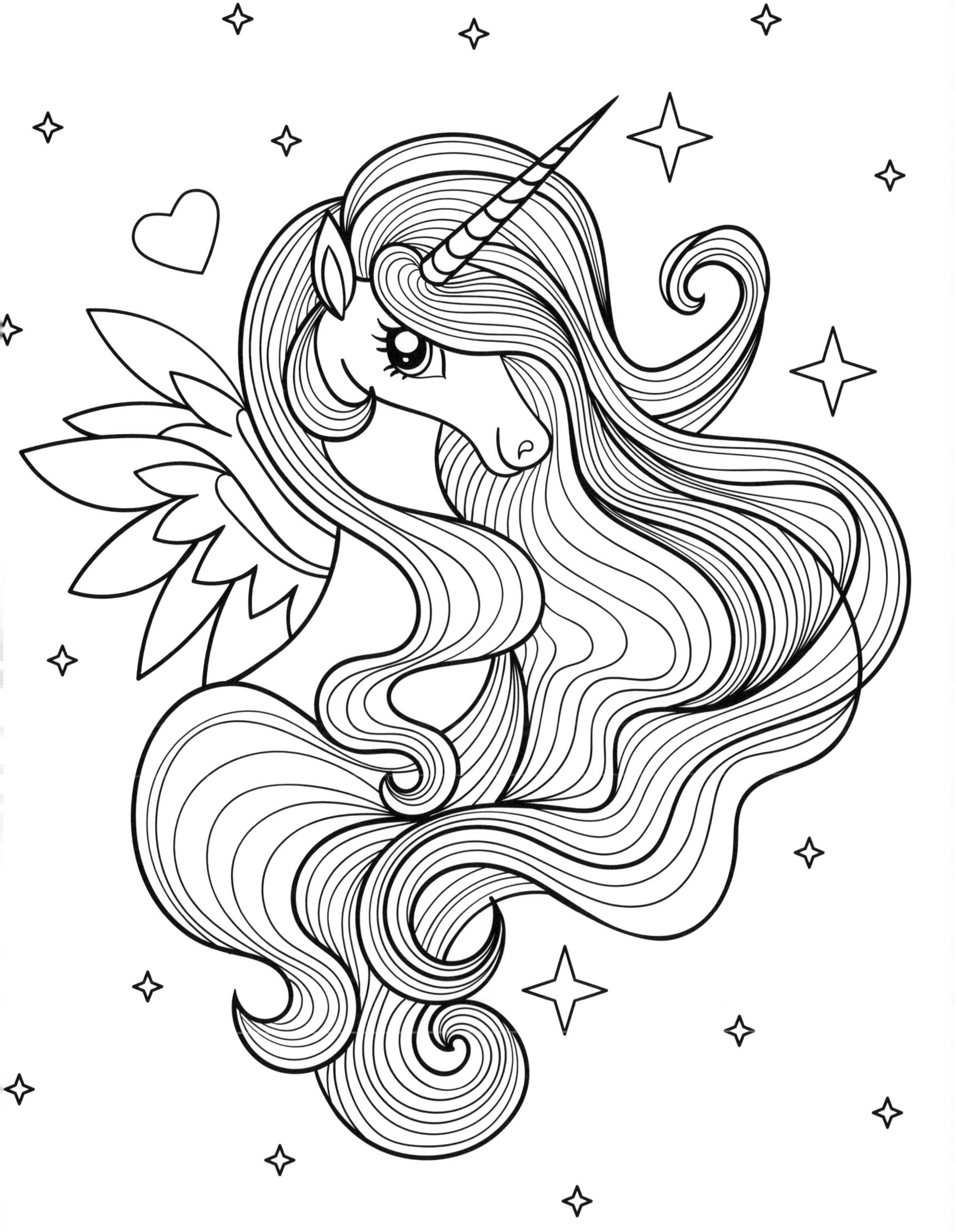

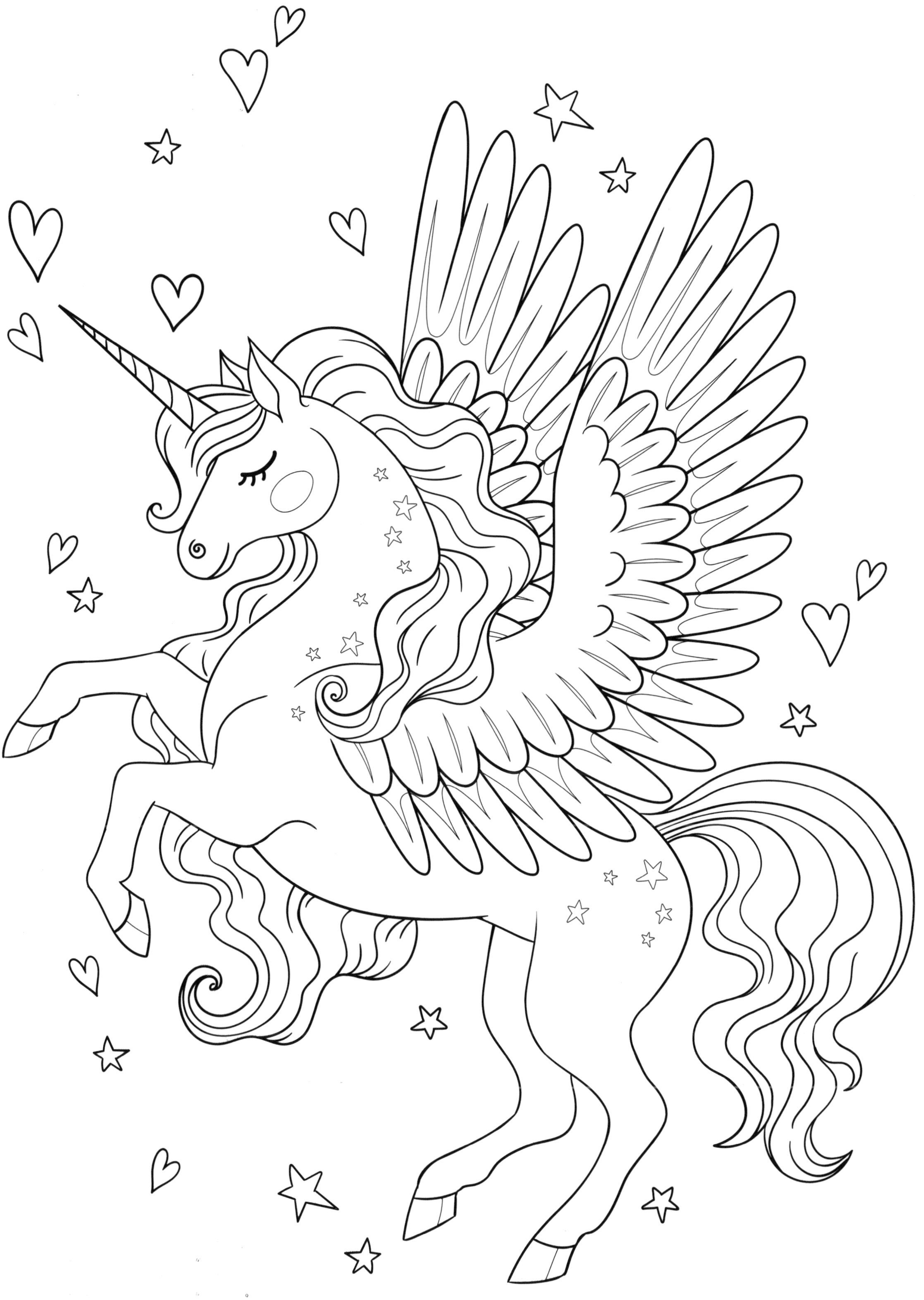

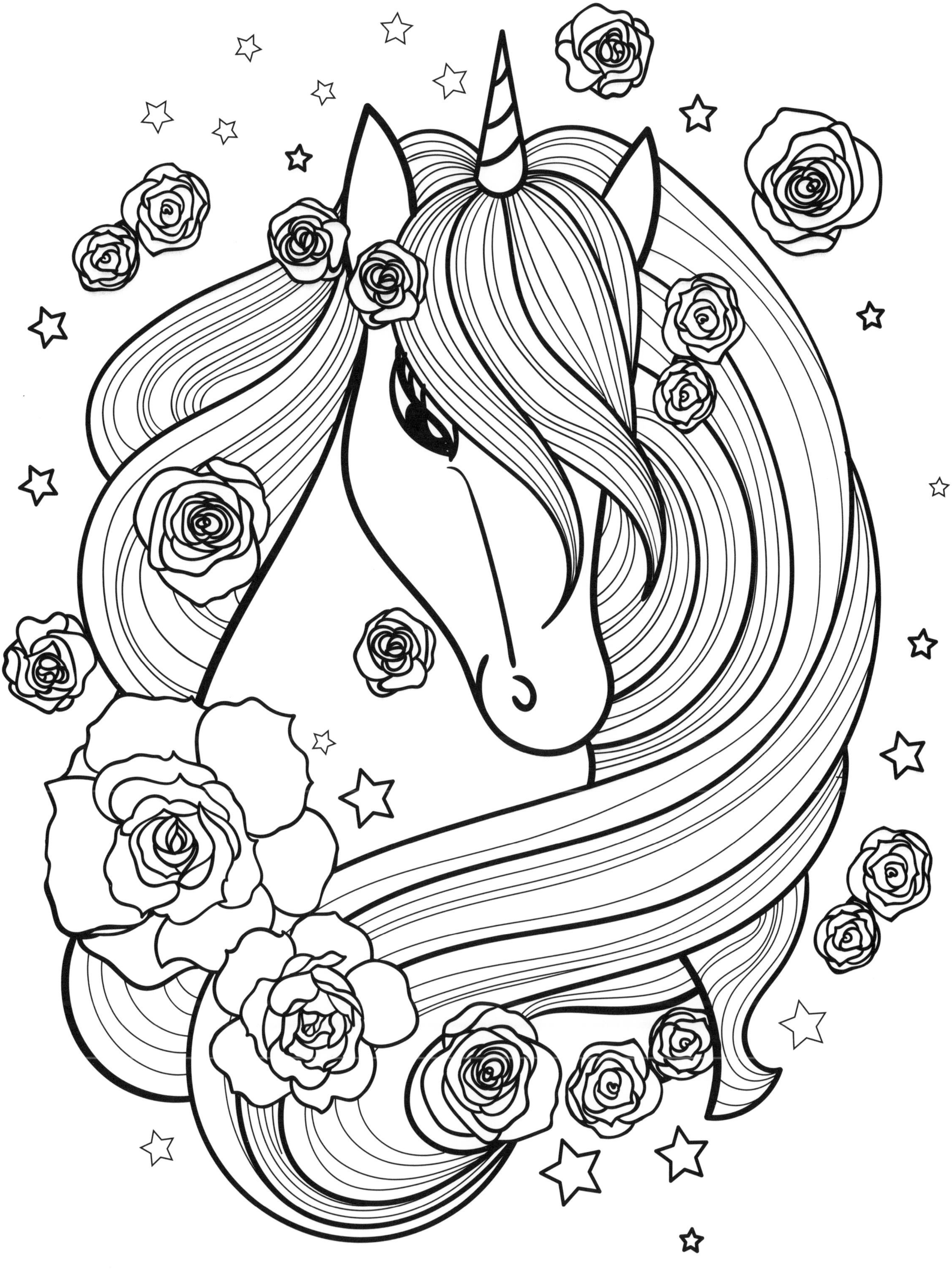

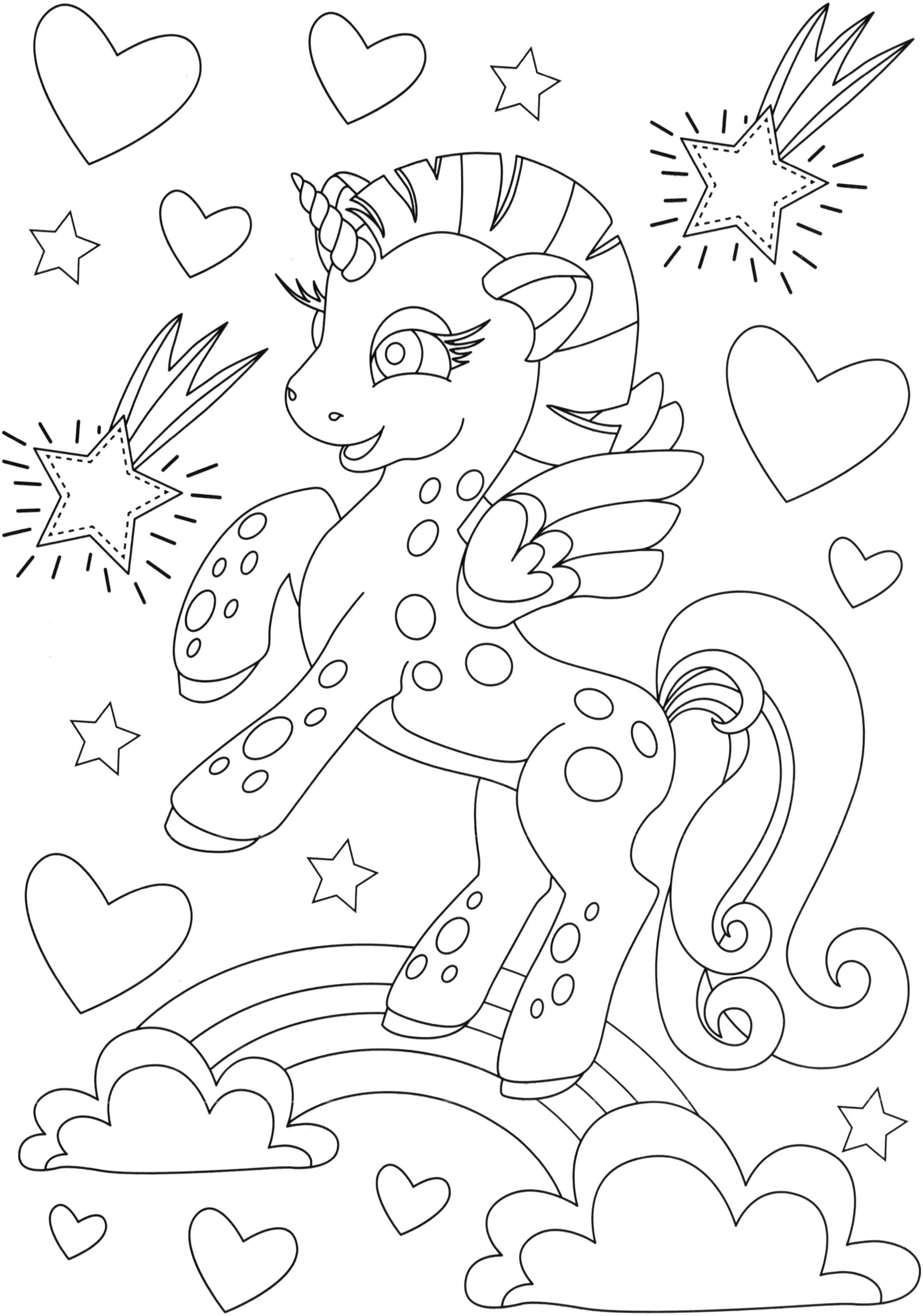

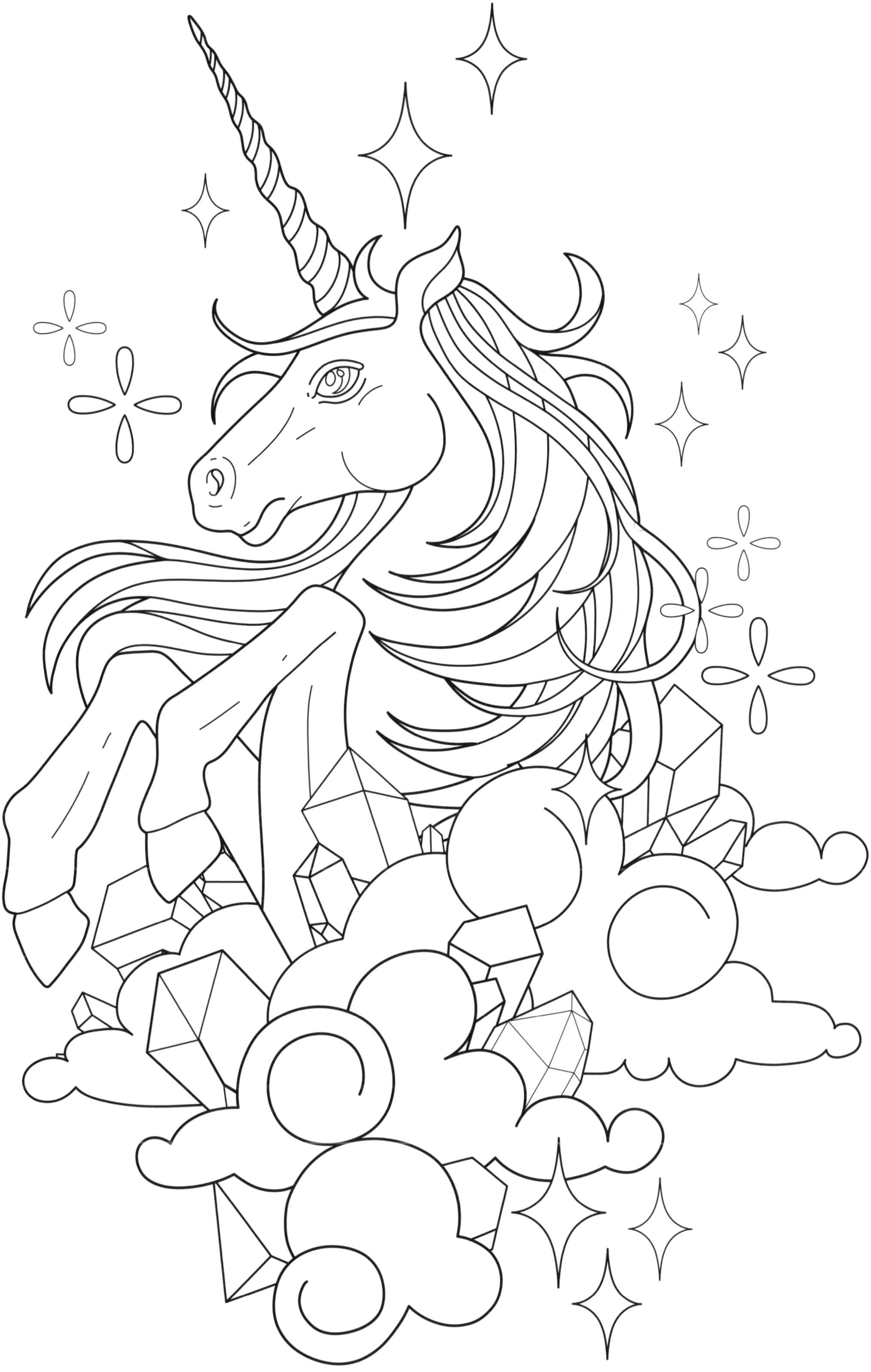

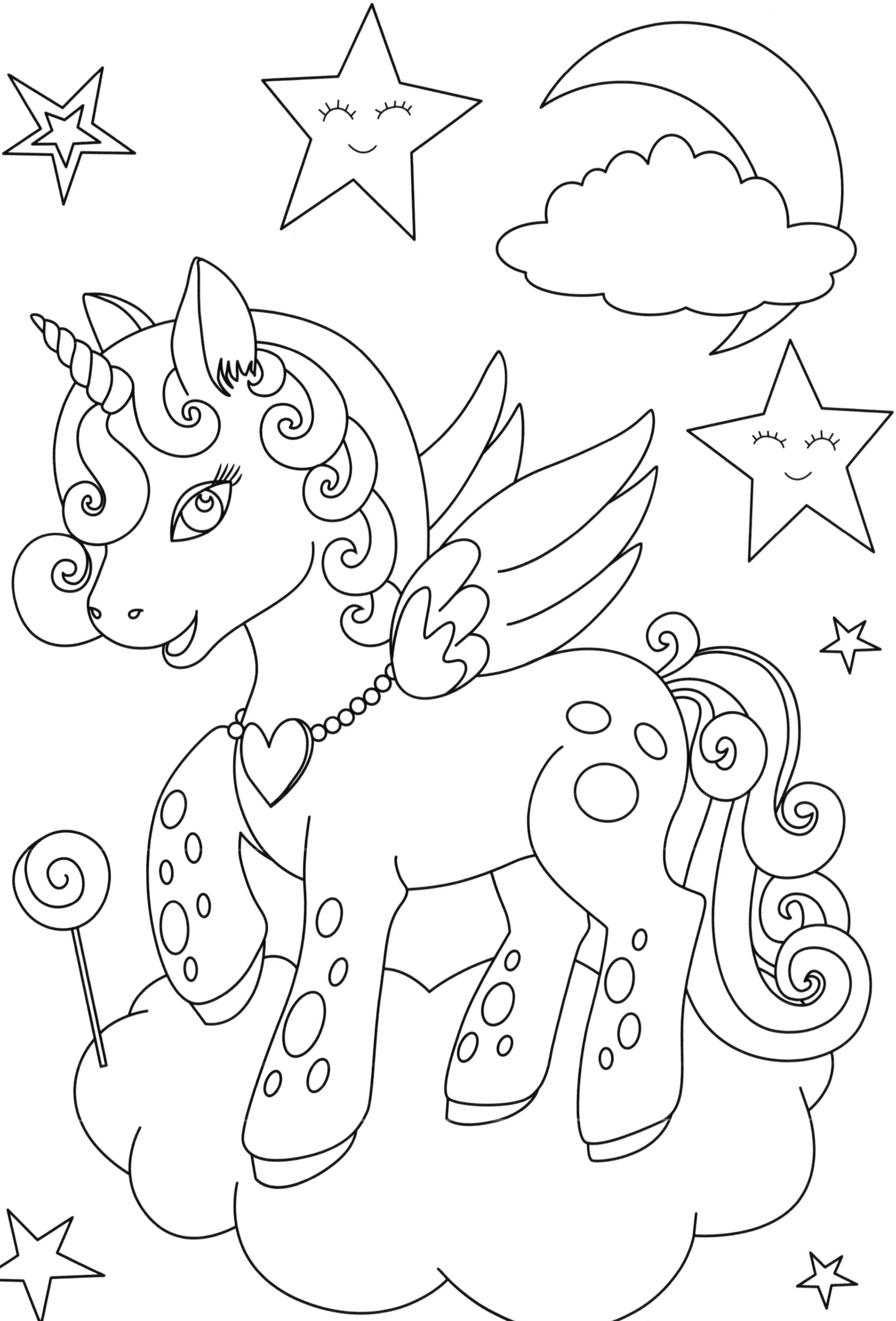

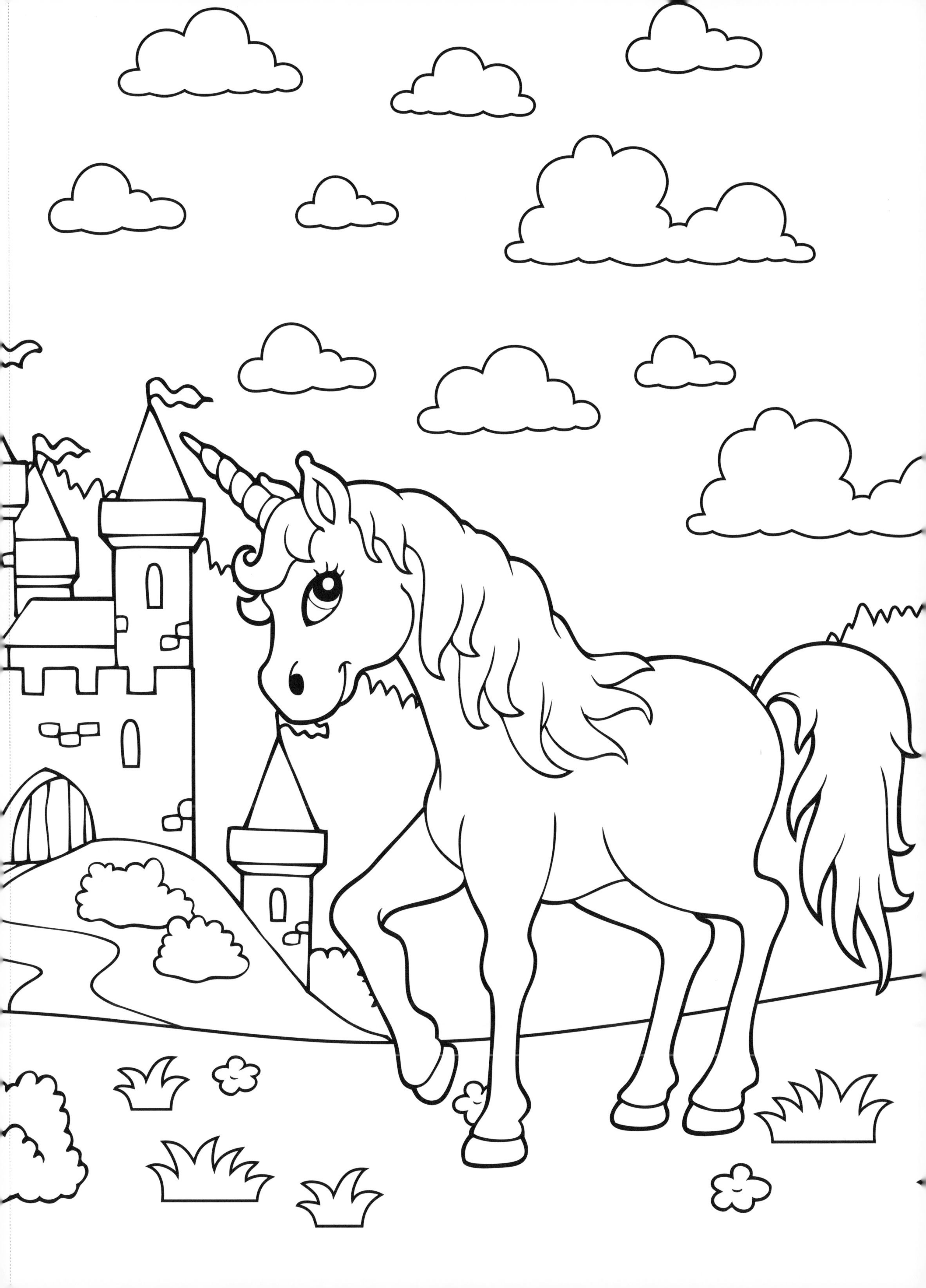

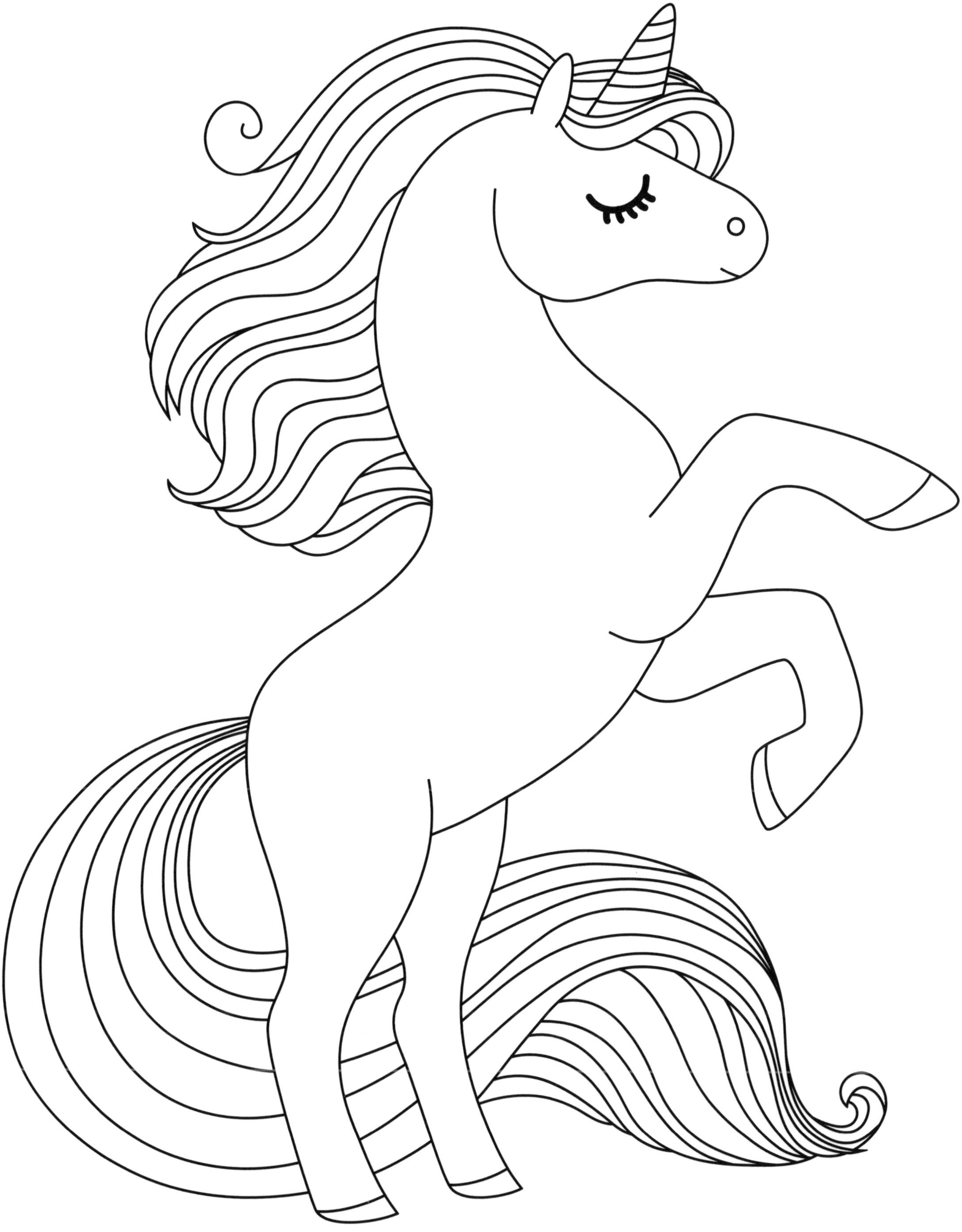

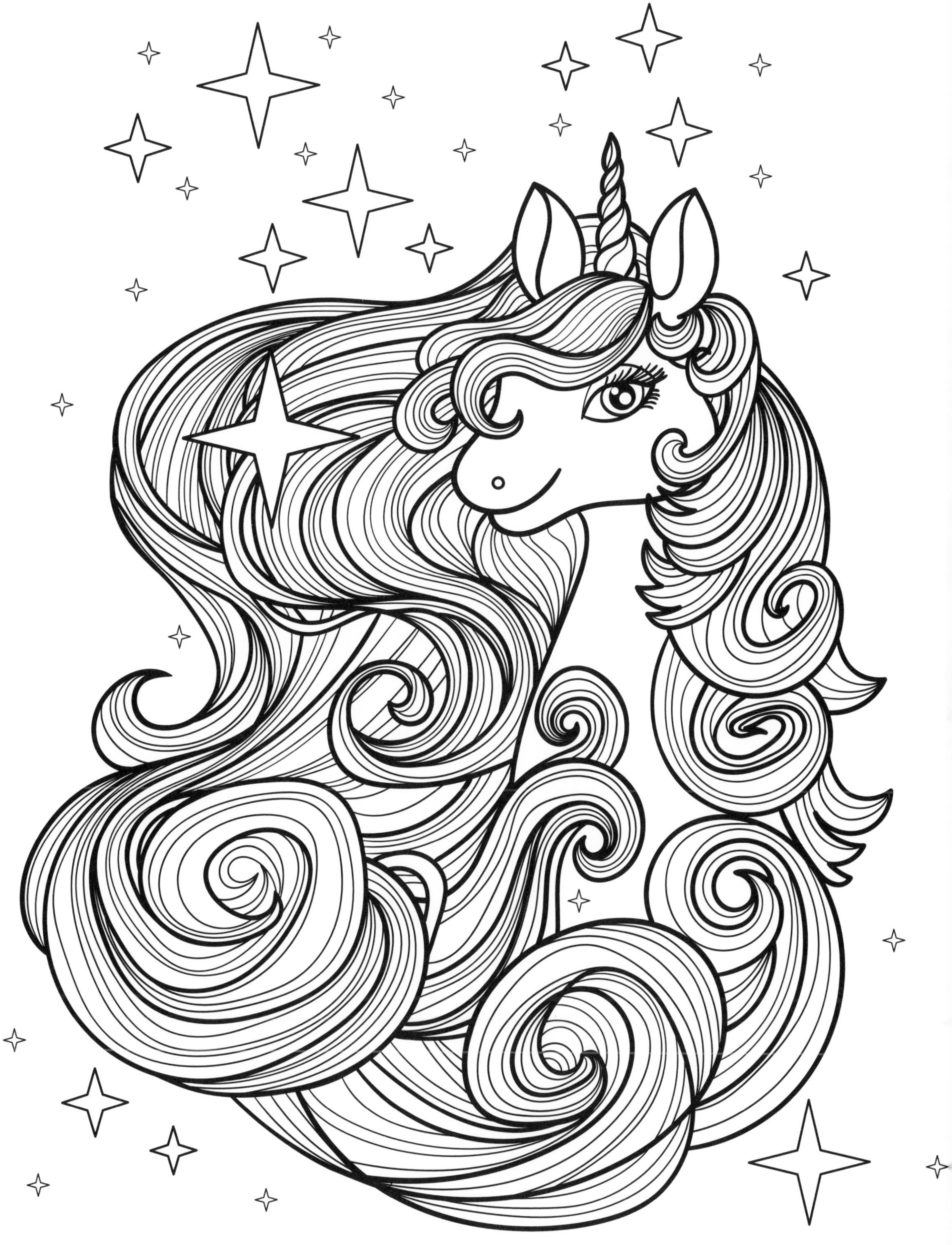

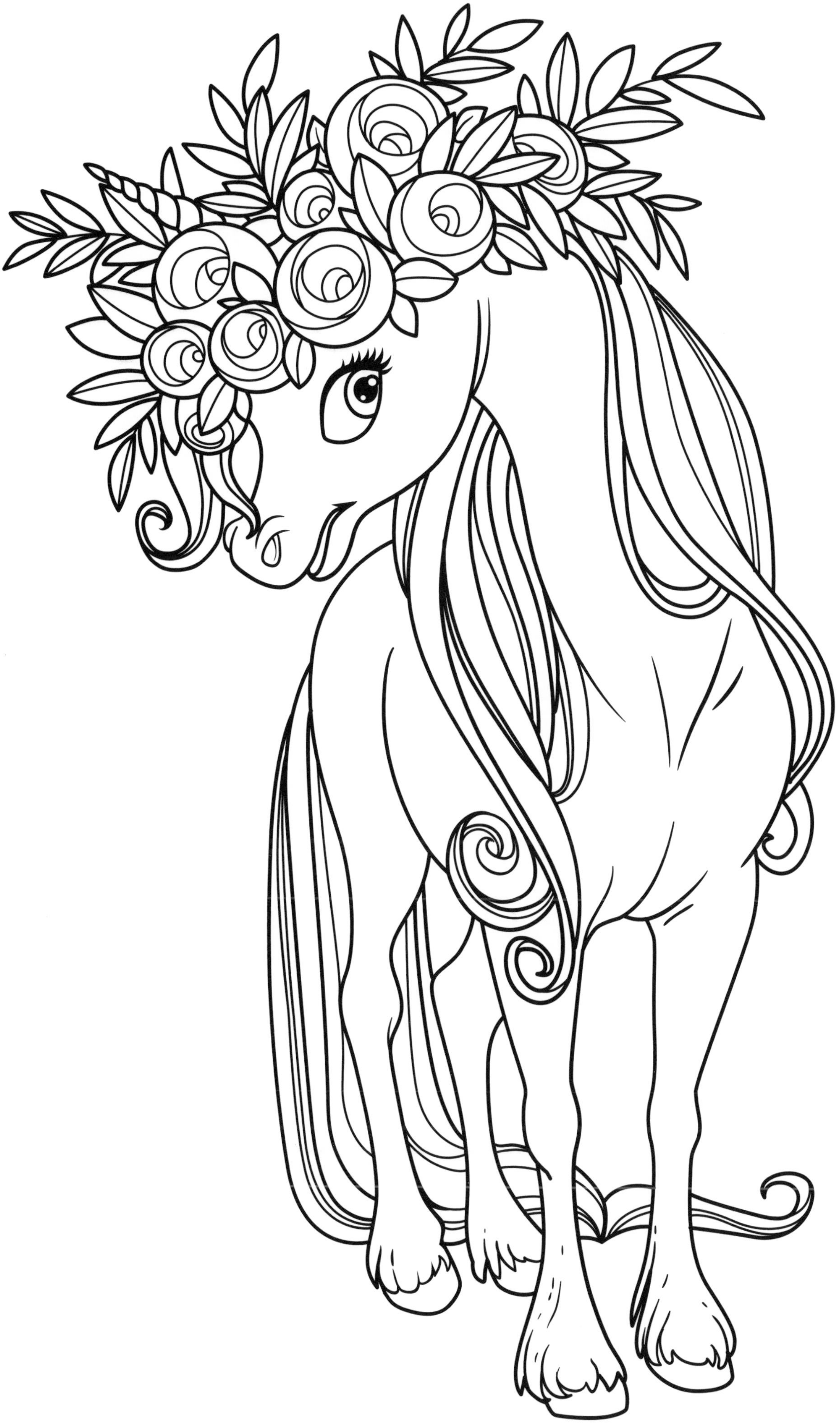

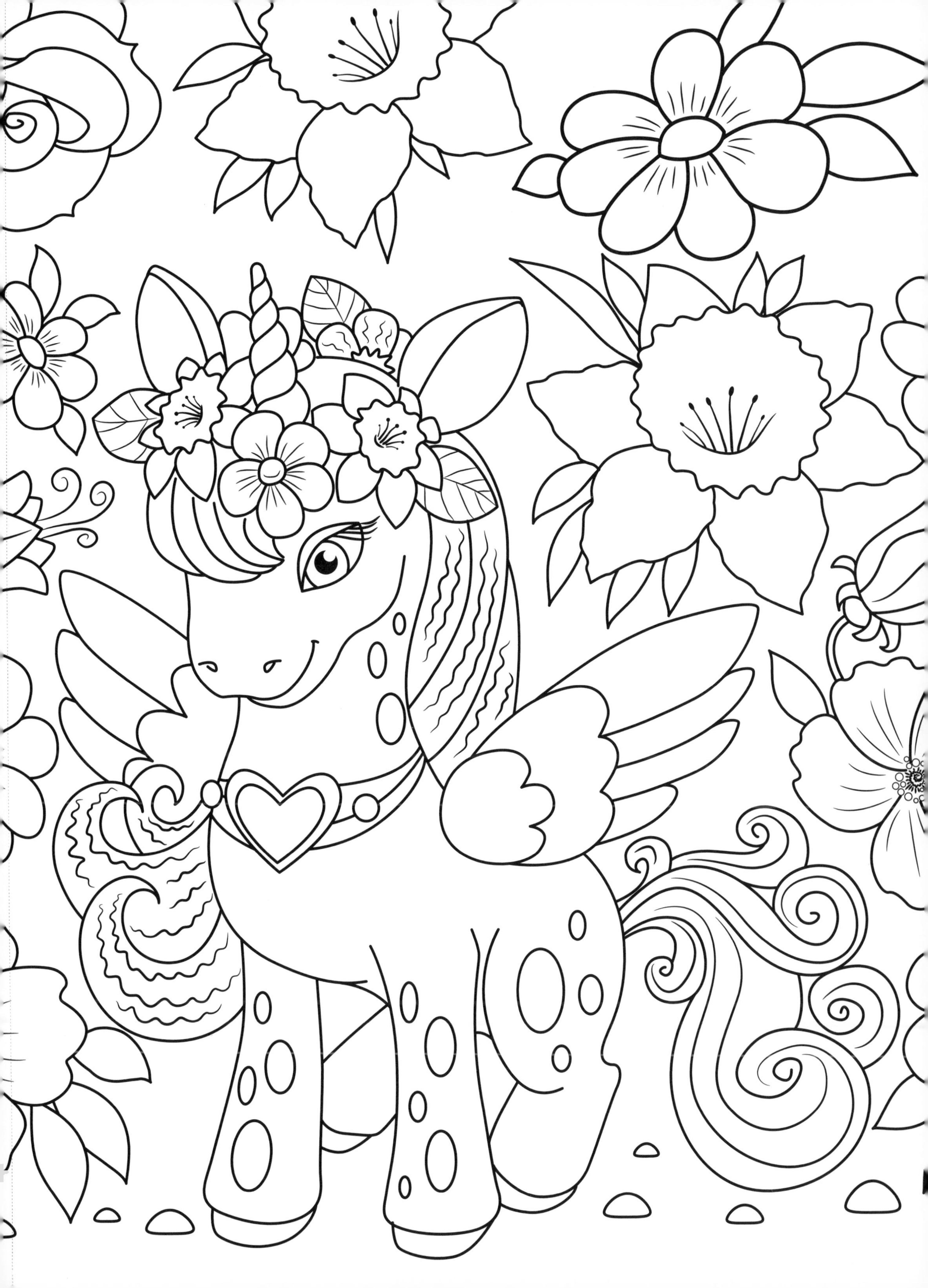

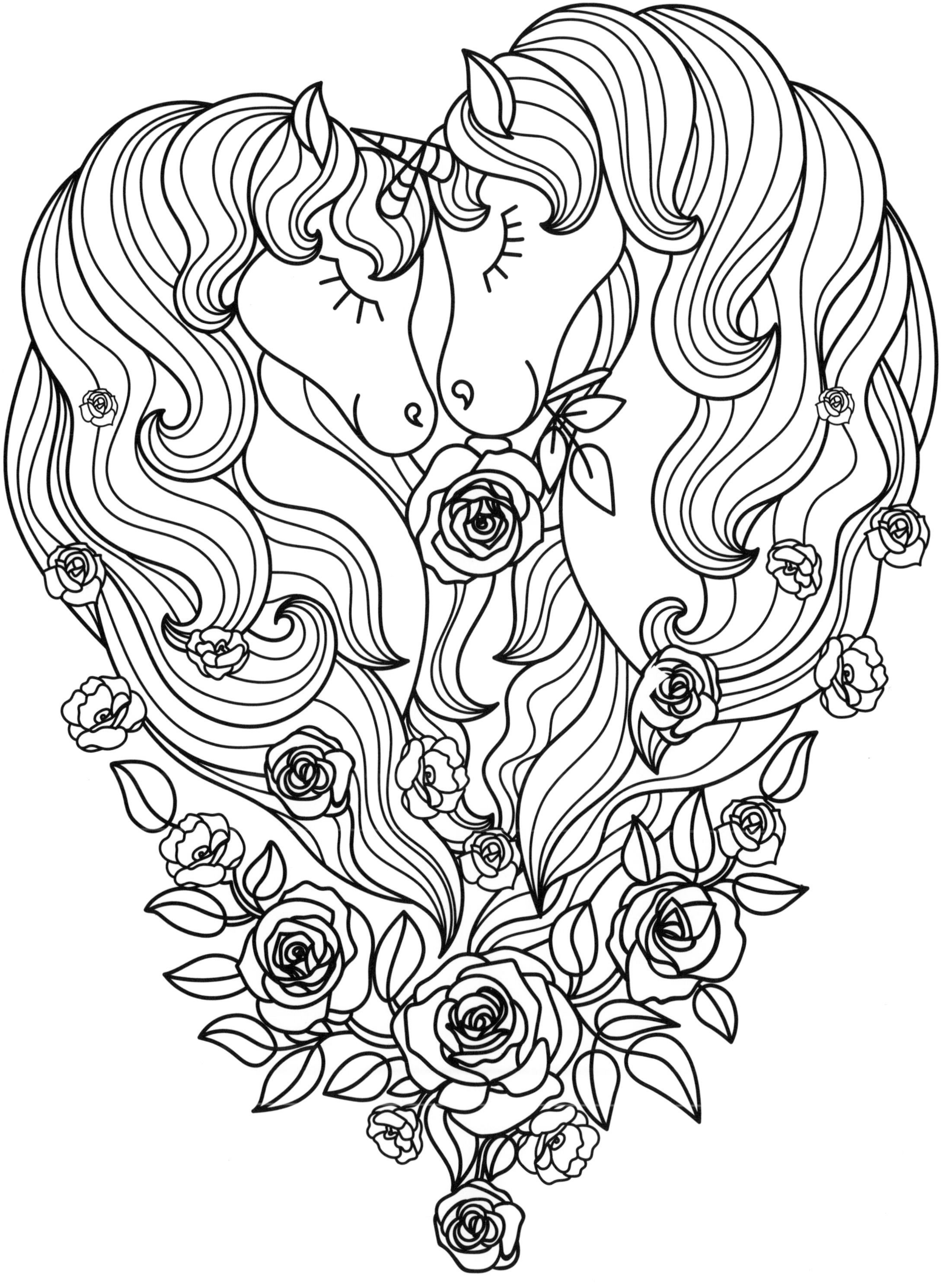